Advanced UFT 12 for Test Engineers Cookbook

Over 60 practical recipes to help you accomplish
automation tasks using UFT 12 and VBScript

Meir Bar-Tal

Jonathon Lee Wright

[PACKT] enterprise
PUBLISHING   professional expertise distilled

BIRMINGHAM - MUMBAI

Advanced UFT 12 for Test Engineers Cookbook

First published: November 2014

Production reference: 1221114

Published by Packt Publishing Ltd.
Livery Place
35 Livery Street
Birmingham B3 2PB, UK.

ISBN 978-1-84968-840-6

www.packtpub.com

Cover image by Faiz F (faizfattohi@gmail.com)

Credits

About the Authors

Meir Bar-Tal holds a Master's Degree in Cognitive Psychology from the Ben-Gurion University of the Negev, but he made a swift switch to the software industry in 2000 and is currently an independent test automation architect. In 2007, Meir was one of the cofounders of the popular knowledge sharing site www.advancedqtp.com (originally founded as a personal blog by Yaron Assa) and has been its Editor in Chief and Forum Administrator ever since (sole owner since 2011). The site's forums were among the final four candidates at the Automated Testing Institute Awards several times, and once were second only to the renowned SQA Forums. Apart from the materials he publishes on his site from time to time, Meir is a regular contributor to several professional online groups and forums and also conducts lectures on UFT at Ness IT Business College (Israel) and other institutions. In 2008, he joined Yaron Assa and others in establishing a small consultancy firm, SOLMAR Knowledge Networks Ltd., which was active until early 2011, when the partners decided to go their separate paths. Since then, Meir worked as an independent freelancer and became a SmartBear Software Authorized Provider. In 2011, he developed a QTP plugin for SeeTest, which enabled interoperability and IntelliSense. In 2014, he joined UGenTech Ltd. as the Associate Director of Automation.

Meir has been involved in many projects characterized by a wide array of technologies (COM, Unix, Windows, Web, .NET, Win Forms, WPF, Java, C#, and so on) and business industries (Derivatives, Banking, Medical, Storage, CRM, Billing, VOIP, and so on). The range of services he provides is wide and includes consultancy, project management, design and development, training and coaching, tools evaluation, and extensibility and plugins development.

Meir has provided services to firms such as HP Software, Experitest, Omnisys, IBM XIV, Hermes Logistics, Bank Leumi, YIT, Ginger Software, and Mazor Robotics. Before he co-found Solmar in 2008, he worked for several companies, including dbMotion, Type Reader, Amdocs, Matrix, and ultimately, Super Derivatives. At Super Derivatives, he led a team of QTP developers to implement an object-oriented framework for QTP, a point that reflects his special interest in the design and development of frameworks and enthusiasm to share the fruits of his research and experience with others. In 2013-2014, he was, as a subcontractor, technical lead of a challenging project at HP Software, in which UFT was used to automate end-to-end scenarios for HP ALM with great success. Besides this, he works in close cooperation with HP Software R&D and periodically contributes his insights to improve UFT.

It would not have been possible to accomplish this piece of work without the assistance (and patience) of several people to whom I wish to express my gratitude and deep appreciation. First and foremost, to my late father who, by his own example, taught me that giving up is not an option; second, to my beloved daughters who always give me strength to accomplish more than what seems feasible; third, to my mother, who has always loved and supported, though not understood, me and all my endeavors; fourth, to my reviewers and editors, who contributed to me personally and to the final quality of this book.

Last, but not least, to all members of Packt Publishing, for giving me this wonderful, exciting, and challenging opportunity to share my knowledge. I wish to extend my special appreciation to Anila Vincent, for her understanding of the difficulties I faced during this project and her virtually unlimited patience, which unfortunately, I was forced to put to the test more than once.

Jonathon Lee Wright has over 15 years of international automation experience with a number of global organizations, including Lehman Brothers, Hitachi Consulting, Siemens, Thomson Reuters, New Zealand Lotteries Commission, PlanIT (Sydney), Unisys (iPSL), Xerox (BJSS), Hewlett Packard (Enterprise), and Microsoft (ALM). Currently, he provides enterprise-wide Portfolio Lifecycle Management at Deutsche Bank as part of the test automation transition initiative, targeting 2,700 applications for test automation across the bank's global digital enterprise landscape/ecosystem.

Jonathon also contributed to the best-selling book *Experiences of Test Automation: Case Studies of Software Test Automation, Dorothy Graham and Mark Fewster, Addison Wesley*, and a number of books on Testing as a Service (TaaS) models (epistemic and systemic entropy) and API testing in the cloud (service and network virtualization). He is the founder of Test Automation as a Service (TaaaS.net) and Automation Development Services (`automation.org.uk`) and the Hybrid approach pattern (2004). He has also presented at various international testing conferences, such as Gartner (London), STARWest (California), Fusion (Sydney), ANZTB (Melbourne), EuroSTAR (Gothenburg and Dublin), BCS SIGIST (London). Further details about Jonathon can be found at `www.linkedin.com/in/automation`.

I would like to thank my father John Wright, without whose support and encouragement none of this would have been possible, for providing the solid foundation for my success over the years. Then, I would like to thank everyone at Packt Publishing, especially Shweta Pant for her support during the technical editing.

About the Reviewers

Seth Eden has a powerful drive to benefit success for the people and organizations that he works with. He began his professional career while still in college, teaching AutoCAD labs, managing the Minnesota State University of Mankato Computer Aided Design archive room, and coordinating design changes and Vikings/Chiefs summer training camp for the NFL. He has worked in a broad spectrum of computer and engineering fields, from mechanical engineering R&D to university labs in Washington, Michigan, and Minnesota. He has written tax-audit management systems for the US Department of Revenue, and most recently worked with mega project engineers on a manufacturing project to support the heavy shipping industry and the offshore oil and gas systems manufacturing at Intergraph. Now, he is working to automate QA testing systems with various insurance companies in Birmingham, Alabama.

Seth is also taking on active research in 3D metal printing and alternative energy systems.

Seth has worked with Trent on a book called *Soul Surviving* with the goal to raise money for the American Cancer Society. He has worked with Dr. Julio Sanchez on a yet unpublished book on Assembly Language programming. He has also been involved in publications with the International Mars Society, documentation on using AutoCAD to model and manage university parking facilities, and processing of Landsat satellite imagery from NASA. You can find more of his work at `Writings.SethEden.com`.

I would like to thank my wife for all the support she has given me through this process. I could never have done it without her!

NaveenKumar Namachivayam has been working as a test analyst with Infosys for the past 8 years. He is highly proficient in automation testing (QTP/UFT), performance testing (LoadRunner, JMeter, CA LISA, and Performance Center), and quality center.

NaveenKumar is a testing professional with strong analytical skills, an aptitude to think innovatively, and troubleshoot problems to meet tight timelines. He blogs at `www.QAInsights.com` about software testing tools. Also, he is an avid learner and experiments with various trends in software testing.

Currently, he is writing a book on MS Excel titled *Excel in MS Excel*, which will release soon.

I would like to thank my parents for providing me with competence and intellect. Also, I would like to thank my wife, Preethi, and my newborn baby daughter, Diya, too.

www.PacktPub.com

Support files, eBooks, discount offers, and more

For support files and downloads related to your book, please visit www.PacktPub.com.

Did you know that Packt offers eBook versions of every book published, with PDF and ePub files available? You can upgrade to the eBook version at www.PacktPub.com and as a print book customer, you are entitled to a discount on the eBook copy. Get in touch with us at service@packtpub.com for more details.

At www.PacktPub.com, you can also read a collection of free technical articles, sign up for a range of free newsletters and receive exclusive discounts and offers on Packt books and eBooks.

https://www2.packtpub.com/books/subscription/packtlib

Do you need instant solutions to your IT questions? PacktLib is Packt's online digital book library. Here, you can search, access, and read Packt's entire library of books.

Why subscribe?

- ▸ Fully searchable across every book published by Packt
- ▸ Copy and paste, print, and bookmark content
- ▸ On demand and accessible via a web browser

Free access for Packt account holders

If you have an account with Packt at www.PacktPub.com, you can use this to access PacktLib today and view 9 entirely free books. Simply use your login credentials for immediate access.

Instant updates on new Packt books

Get notified! Find out when new books are published by following @PacktEnterprise on Twitter or the *Packt Enterprise* Facebook page.

Table of Contents

Preface

Unlock the full potential of Unified Functional Testing (UFT) 12 with the introduction of new features and functionality. Learn the industry's best kept secrets, enhancing toolset capabilities like you never thought possible. Whether you are a casual user of UFT or an advanced power user searching for new automation design patterns to supercharge your existing framework, look no further as this is the book for you.

Join the authors who, with three decades of automation expertise between them, are ready to share with you ways to make your tests more relevant, effective, maintainable, efficient, manageable, portable, and reliable. This book is designed to be an invaluable source of reference for everyone with its clear and powerful coding examples. Why waste any more time trying to reinvent the wheel? Instead, accelerate straight to the expert level in UFT today!

What this book covers

Chapter 1, *Data-driven Tests*, covers the design patterns required to truly unlock the DataTable functionalities (create, retrieve, store, import, and export).

Chapter 2, *Testing Web Pages*, covers the design patterns required to manage modern-day browser capabilities and the challenges: handling broken links, websites' downtime, multiple browser instances, cookies, unexpected pop-ups, downloading and uploading files, synchronization, and most importantly, object identification and checking dynamic content through the DOM.

Chapter 3, *Testing XML and Database*, covers the design patterns required to manage DB connections, executing SQL statements, and a walkthrough of advanced DB and XML checkpoints.

Chapter 4, *Method Overriding*, covers the design patterns required to override a Test Object method, enriching basic functions, and adding exception handling mechanisms.

Chapter 5, *Object Identification*, covers the design patterns required to effectively manage the object identification process through techniques such as Inline Descriptive Programming, Description Object, ChildObjects, and native properties.

Chapter 6, *Event and Exception Handling*, covers the design patterns required to provide robust and maintainable tests that can deal with unexpected events or exceptions by catching errors inside a function or subroutine, recovery scenarios, and how to use the global dictionary for recovery.

Chapter 7, *Using Classes*, covers the design patterns required to implement classes in VBScript, along with illustrative examples and implementing function pointers.

Chapter 8, *Utility and Reserved Objects*, covers the design patterns required to utilize advanced functionality hidden within the depths of UFT.

Chapter 9, *Windows Script Host*, covers the design patterns surrounding the underlying infrastructure provided by the platform to execute scripts written in a variety of programming languages.

Chapter 10, *Frameworks*, covers the design patterns to implement modern-day test automation frameworks exploring modular-driven, data-driven, keyword-driven, model-driven, and hybrid techniques to find the best approach that works for you.

Appendix, *Design Patterns*, covers the additional design patterns, including auxiliary classes and functions, to enhance the tool set capabilities and unlock the full potential of UFT. It provides powerful examples for both the action and runtime data patterns to put into practice what has been covered in the previous chapters.

What you will need for this book

The only prerequisite for this book is that you need the latest version of HP's UFT installed. This can be downloaded directly from the HP enterprise website:

```
http://www8.hp.com/uk/en/software-solutions/unified-functional-
testing-automation/
```

The example code design patterns snippets are for reference only and need to be adapted to become context-driven.

To add example code files to the UFT solution:

1. From the project navigate to **File** | **Settings**.
2. Click on the **Resources** section.
3. Click on the **+** button, then the ellipses button on the far right to browse to the location where the function library is located.
4. Navigate to the location of the example code file and click on **Open** to associate to the project resources.
5. Then a pop-up message will present itself with **Automatic Relative Path Conversion** at which point you can decide to use a Absolute Path or Relative Path.

Alternatively, right-click on the test project and navigate to **Add | Associate Function Library** to fast track the above process.

Who this book is for

This book is designed to be an invaluable source of reference for end users of HP's UFT.

Depending on your exposure level to coding with VBScript, you may require assistance with some of the more advanced design patterns.

Sections

Each chapter contains sections using the following structure:

Getting ready

This section tells us what to expect in the recipe and describes how to set up any software or any preliminary settings needed for the recipe.

How to do it...

This section characterizes the steps to be followed for "cooking" the recipe.

How it works...

This section usually consists of a brief and detailed explanation of what happened in the previous section.

There's more...

It consists of additional information about the recipe in order to make the reader more confident about using the recipe.

See also

This section will, where needed, contain additional references to the recipe.

Conventions

In this book, you will find a number of styles of text that distinguish between different kinds of information. Here are some examples of these styles, and an explanation of their meaning.

Code words in text, database table names, folder names, filenames, file extensions, pathnames, dummy URLs, user input, and Twitter handles are shown as follows: "We will retrieve the value of a `DataTable` parameter, namely, `LocalParam1`, from the `Action1` local sheet with the following code written in the code editor inside `Action1`"

A block of code is set as follows:

```
Dim MyLocalParam

MyLocalParam = DataTable.Value("LocalParam1", dtLocalSheet)
Print MyLocalParam
```

New terms and **important words** are shown in bold. Words that you see on the screen, in menus or dialog boxes for example, appear in the text like this: "Leave all the fields with the default values and click on **OK**."

Warnings or important notes appear in a box like this.

Tips and tricks appear like this.

Reader feedback

Feedback from our readers is always welcome. Let us know what you think about this book—what you liked or may have disliked. Reader feedback is important for us to develop titles that you really get the most out of.

To send us general feedback, simply send an e-mail to feedback@packtpub.com, and mention the book title via the subject of your message.

If there is a topic that you have expertise in and you are interested in either writing or contributing to a book, see our author guide on www.packtpub.com/authors.

Customer support

Now that you are the proud owner of a Packt book, we have a number of things to help you to get the most from your purchase.

Downloading the example code

You can download the example code files for all Packt books you have purchased from your account at http://www.packtpub.com. If you purchased this book elsewhere, you can visit http://www.packtpub.com/support and register to have the files e-mailed directly to you.

Errata

Although we have taken every care to ensure the accuracy of our content, mistakes do happen. If you find a mistake in one of our books—maybe a mistake in the text or the code—we would be grateful if you would report this to us. By doing so, you can save other readers from frustration and help us improve subsequent versions of this book. If you find any errata, please report them by visiting `http://www.packtpub.com/submit-errata`, selecting your book, clicking on the **errata submission form** link, and entering the details of your errata. Once your errata are verified, your submission will be accepted and the errata will be uploaded on our website, or added to any list of existing errata, under the Errata section of that title. Any existing errata can be viewed by selecting your title from `http://www.packtpub.com/support`.

Piracy

Piracy of copyright material on the Internet is an ongoing problem across all media. At Packt, we take the protection of our copyright and licenses very seriously. If you come across any illegal copies of our works, in any form, on the Internet, please provide us with the location address or website name immediately so that we can pursue a remedy.

Please contact us at `copyright@packtpub.com` with a link to the suspected pirated material.

We appreciate your help in protecting our authors, and our ability to bring you valuable content.

Questions

You can contact us at `questions@packtpub.com` if you are having a problem with any aspect of the book, and we will do our best to address it.

1

Data-driven Tests

In this chapter, we will cover the following recipes:

- ▶ Creating a DataTable parameter
- ▶ Retrieving data from a DataTable
- ▶ Storing data in a DataTable
- ▶ Importing an Excel file to a test
- ▶ Exporting a DataTable
- ▶ Parameterizing Test Object properties
- ▶ Defining test cases using a DataTable
- ▶ Storing data in the Environment object
- ▶ Retrieving data from the Environment object
- ▶ Reading values from an INI file
- ▶ Using a configuration file to manage test environments
- ▶ Using a global dictionary for fast shared data access
- ▶ Using a global dictionary for fast shared code access

Introduction

This chapter describes several ways by which data can be used to drive automated tests in UFT. Data-driven tests enable us to cover different paths in a test flow, by supplying a coded script with different sets of values to its parameters. These include input data for manipulating GUI objects and, where relevant, also the expected output from the application under test. In other words, a data-driven script is one whose behavior changes when fed with different sets of input data.

We can retrieve input data using the global `DataTable` object. The first seven recipes explain how we can work with a DataTable to attain various goals related to the concept of data-driven tests. The next two recipes deal with Environment variables using the `Environment` object. The *Reading values from an INI file* and *Using a configuration file to manage test environments* recipes show how to retrieve values from INI files and how to manage test environments with them. Finally, the *Using a global dictionary for fast shared data access* and *Using a global dictionary for fast shared code access* recipes describe advanced techniques for fast shared data and code access using a `Dictionary` object.

 When we work with a DataTable in UFT, we must keep in mind that an action datasheet always carries the same name as the associated action, and that its data is visible only to the action.

Creating a DataTable parameter

`DataTable` is a UFT object that acts as a wrapper to an MS Excel file, and its scope is global. This means that it can be accessed from any action within a test, as well as from function libraries that were attached to the test. When you create a new test or open an existing UFT test, you will notice that the DataTable pane will always show a global and local datasheet, one for each existing action within the test. In this section, we will see how to create a DataTable parameter.

How to do it...

Perform the following steps to create the DataTable parameter `LocalParam1` for the local sheet:

1. From the **File** menu, navigate to **New | Test** or use the *Ctrl + N* shortcut. When a new test dialog opens, choose **GUI Test** and then click on the **Create** button.

2. We will create a DataTable parameter in the `Action1` local sheet from the UFT data pane by double-clicking on the column header and entering the parameter name `LocalParam1` in the dialog that opens, as shown in the following screenshot:

Similarly, for the test global sheet we will create a parameter named `GlobalParam1`.

3. Next, we need to enter our input data in the remaining cells of the parameter column in the global or local sheet, according to the requirements.

How it works...

If we open the `Default.xls` file in the `test` folder (which, as its name suggests, is the default data source for a new test), we will notice that there are two worksheets, namely, `Global` and `Action1`. In each of these, the first row holds the name of the parameters, so we will see `GlobalParam1` in the `Global` worksheet and `LocalParam1` in the `Action1` worksheet. You will also notice that the used rows have borders at the bottom of the worksheet (the borders have no real function; UFT identifies the used range by the number of used rows and columns based on the content range).

See also

For information about setting and retrieving values for a DataTable parameter, refer to the next two recipes, *Retrieving data from a DataTable* and *Storing data in a DataTable*.

Retrieving data from a DataTable

`DataTable` is a UFT object that acts as a wrapper to an MS Excel file, and its scope is global. This means that it can be accessed from any action within a test, as well as from function libraries that were attached to the test. When you create a new test or open an existing UFT test, you will notice that the DataTable pane will always show a global datasheet and a local one for each existing action within the test.

Getting ready

Prior to getting started with this recipe, please ensure that you have followed the *Creating a DataTable parameter* recipe.

How to do it...

We will retrieve the value of a DataTable parameter, namely, `LocalParam1`, from the `Action1` local sheet with the following code written in the code editor inside `Action1`:

```
Dim MyLocalParam

MyLocalParam = DataTable.Value("LocalParam1", dtLocalSheet)
Print MyLocalParam
```

Similarly, the following code snippet shows how to retrieve the value of a DataTable parameter from the test global sheet:

```
Dim MyGlobalParam
MyGlobalParam = DataTable("GlobalParam1", dtGlobalSheet)
'We can omit the explicit .Value property as given above since it is
the default property
Print MyGlobalParam
MyGlobalParam = DataTable("GlobalParam1")
'We can omit the second parameter as given above (dtGlobalSheet) since
the Global sheet is the default
Print MyGlobalParam
```

Downloading the example code

You can download the example code files for all Packt books you have purchased from your account at http://www.packtpub.com. If you purchased this book elsewhere, you can visit http://www.packtpub.com/support and register to have the files e-mailed directly to you.

The result of this code in UFT's console is as follows:

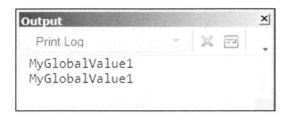

Of course, we need to ensure beforehand that the parameter exists in the DataTable class as outlined in the previous *Creating a DataTable parameter* recipe.

How it works...

By using the DataTable.Value property we are referring to the column by the parameter name in the underlying Excel worksheet (be it global or local):

```
MyLocalParam = DataTable.Value("LocalParam1", dtLocalSheet)
MyGlobalParam = DataTable("GlobalParam1", dtGlobalSheet)
```

As we entered just a single value into the datasheet, the command retrieves just the value in the first row. If multiple values were entered and action iterations were set to run on all rows, then it would have retrieved the values from each row with each iteration.

 The `dtLocalSheet` constant always refers to the datasheet by the name of the current action. The `dtGlobalSheet` constant always refers to the global datasheet and can be used in any action.

Storing data in a DataTable

Sometimes, data that is collected during a run session might be needed for later use. For example, suppose that **Application Under Test** (**AUT**) is a mobile operator management system. We could begin by executing a customer creation process, during which a customer ID is assigned automatically by the system. We then proceed with the other operations, such as selecting a phone number, an IMEI, credit card details, and so on. Later, we may wish to retrieve the customer records and update some personal data such as the mailing address. For this purpose, we will keep the customer ID in the global datasheet, so that any action that is executed, which can be referenced later (for example, one that performs a customer search), will have access to the data.

 Data stored in the global datasheet is effective only until the test stops. To see how to save data persistently for later run sessions, please refer to the *Exporting a DataTable* and *Importing an Excel file to a test* recipes.

How to do it...

Proceed with the following steps:

1. From the **File** menu, select **New | Test** or use the *Ctrl + N* shortcut. When the new test dialog opens, choose **GUI Test** and click on the **Create** button.

2. We will save the value of a DataTable parameter, `CustomerID`, to the global sheet with the following code written in the code editor inside `Action1`:

```
Dim CustomerID

DataTable.GlobalSheet.AddParameter "CustomerID",
    "990011234"
CustomerID = DataTable("CustomerID")
Print Environment("ActionName") & ": " & CustomerID
```

3. To retrieve the value from another action, we will now create a new action datasheet. In the code editor, right-click on the next empty line and select **Action | Call to New Action**, as shown in the following screenshot:

The following dialog will open:

4. Leave all the fields with the default values and click on **OK**. You will see that a new action named `Action2` will appear in the **Solution Explorer** window and open on the code editor's MDI region:

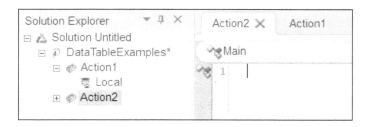

5. Now, we will retrieve the value of the `CustomerID` parameter from the global sheet with the following code inside `Action2`:

```
Dim CustomerID

CustomerID = DataTable("CustomerID")
Print Environment("ActionName") & ": " & CustomerID
```

The result of this code in the UFT's console is shown in the following screenshot:

How it works...

When we run the test, UFT first executes `Action1`, and a new parameter named `CustomerID` will be added to `GlobalSheet` (a property of the `DataTable` object that refers to the `GlobalSheet` object) with the value given by the second parameter.

```
DataTable.GlobalSheet.AddParameter "CustomerID", "990011234"
```

We then immediately assign a variable with the retrieved value and print it to the console (for illustration purposes, we also concatenate the current action's name from the `Environment` object's built-in variables).

```
CustomerID = DataTable("CustomerID")
Print Environment("ActionName") & ": " & CustomerID
```

Next, UFT executes `Action2` same as `Action1`.

There's more...

There are other alternative ways of keeping and sharing data during a run session. The simplest is by using public variables declared in a function library attached to the test. The disadvantage of this approach is that these variables must be declared in advance and they are hard coded, but the nature of automation often demands more flexibility to manage such data.

See also

For information on advanced methods to share data among sessions, refer to the *Using a global dictionary for fast shared data access* recipe.

Importing an Excel file to a test

We can dynamically set the underlying Excel file that will serve as a data source for the whole run session, though this is probably a very rare case, and even switch between such files during the run session. It is possible to import a whole Excel workbook for a test or just a single worksheet for a specific action.

The classical case of importing an Excel file to a test is when the same flow needs to be executed on different environments, such as with multilingual systems. In such a case, the test would require an external parameter to identify the environment, and then load the correct Excel file. Another possibility is that the test identifies the language dynamically, for example, by retrieving the runtime property value of a **Test Object** (**TO**), which indicates the current language, or by retrieving the `lang` attribute of a web page or element.

Getting ready

Ensure that a new test is open and create a new action. Ensure that an external Excel sheet exists with one global worksheet and worksheets named after each action in the test. The Excel sheet will contain three worksheets, namely, `Global`, `Action1`, and `Action2`. The `Action2` worksheet will contain data shown in the following screenshot. In our example, we will use the Excel sheet named `MyDynamicallyLoadedExcel.xls`, and to simplify matters, we will put it under the same test folder (it should be placed in a separate shared folder):

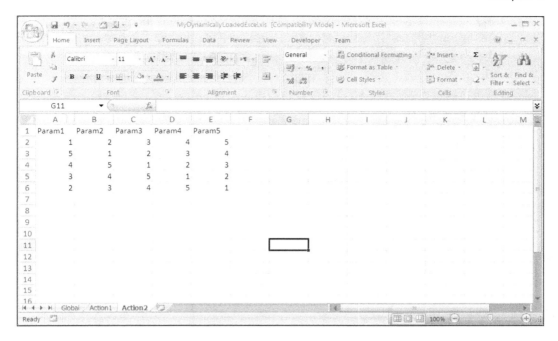

In the **Flow** pane, make sure that the **Action Call** properties are set to **Run on all rows**.

How to do it...

In order to load the `MyDynamicallyLoadedExcel.xls` file to the test, perform the following steps:

1. We use the `DataTable.Import` method to load the Excel sheet. In `Action1` (the first to be run), we use the following code to ensure that the Excel file is loaded only once (to avoid loading Excel for each iteration in case the test is set to **Run on all rows**):

```
Print "Test Iteration #" & Environment("TestIteration") & "
  - " & Environment("ActionName") & " - Action Iteration #"
  & Environment("ActionIteration")
if cint(Environment("TestIteration")) = 1 then
    DataTable.Import("MyDynamicallyLoadedExcel.xls")
end if
```

2. In `Action2`, we use the following code to retrieve the values for all parameters defined in the local datasheet for `Action2`. We first print the number of the current action iteration, so that we may distinguish between the outputs in the console.

```
Print Environment("ActionName") & " - Action Iteration #" &
    Environment("ActionIteration")
For p = 1 to DataTable.LocalSheet.GetParameterCount
    print DataTable.LocalSheet.GetParameter(p)
Next
```

3. When a test is set to **Run on all rows**, it means that it will be executed repeatedly for each row having data in `GlobalSheet`.

The output to the console looks like the following screenshot:

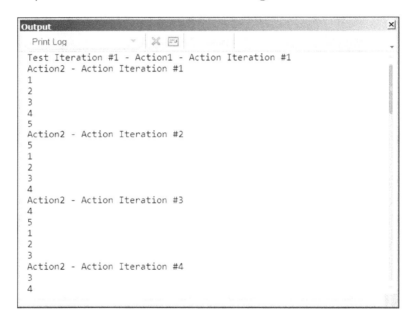

How it works...

In `Action1`, the `DataTable.Import` method replaces `Default.xls` with the target Excel file. The code in `Action2` retrieves and prints the values for each parameter, and as the action was set to **Run on all rows**, the code repeats this for all rows with data.

There's more...

To import just a worksheet for an action, use the `DataTable.ImportSheet` method as follows:

```
DataTable.ImportSheet("MyDynamicallyLoadedExcel.xls", "Action1",
    "Action1")
```

Here, the first parameter is the Excel filename and the last two are the source datasheet and target datasheet respectively.

See also

For information on saving values collected during a run session, refer to the next recipe, *Exporting a DataTable*.

Exporting a DataTable

We may need to save data that is collected during a run session. For example, a comparison of the current result with previous results might be required. Alternatively, we might wish to update the expected results. In such scenarios, we can save the data to an external Excel sheet for later use.

How to do it...

To save the DataTable in its current state before the run session ends, we will use the `DataTable.Export` method, which takes the path and name of an Excel file as an argument. There are two options to save the data table:

▶ Using a hardcoded filename:

```
DataTable.Export(Environment("TestDir") &
    "\MyDynamicallySavedExcel.xls")
```

▶ Using a variable filename:

```
DataTable.Export(Environment("TestDir") & "\" & strFileName
    & ".xls")
```

How it works...

The preceding statement saves the current contents of the DataTable (all worksheets) to a new Excel file (if not existent, otherwise it is overwritten). The statement `Environment("TestDir")` returns a string with the path of the current test to which a string with the name of the file we wish to create is concatenated (`TestDir` is one of the built-in Environment variables covered in detail later in this chapter).

There's more...

To export just a single worksheet (in our example, the global sheet) for an action, use the `DataTable.ExportSheet` method, as follows:

```
call DataTable.ExportSheet(Environment("TestDir") &
   "\MyDynamicallySavedSheet1.xls", "Global")
```

Here, the first parameter is the Excel filename and the second is the source datasheet. The target datasheet will take the same name as the source.

Parameterizing Test Object properties

The same TOs might appear in different flavors. For example, a **Submit** button in a localized English version would show the text **Einreichen** for the German version. If the objects were given abstract IDs not related to their function or displayed text, then life for the automation developer would be easy; however, this is generally not the case. As managing a separate object repository for each language would pose a maintenance impasse for any automation project, a more practical approach should be adopted. A good alternative is to store the values for identification properties that change from one environment to another in an external data source, which is loaded at the beginning of a run session according to the required language. This recipe will show how to parameterize an identification property for a given TO and use the dynamically loaded value to identify the object during runtime.

How to do it...

In this recipe, we will take the Google+ **Sign In** button, which carries a different text value for each localized version. In our example, we will learn about the button in one language (Afrikaans), store the TO in a single **Object Repository** (**OR**), and make it get the value for its `name` attribute from an Environment variable named `Google_Sign_In`. The Environment variables for the test will be loaded according to the application language (refer to the *Using global variables (Environment)* recipe in *Chapter 8, Utility and Reserved Objects*).

Proceed with the following steps:

1. With UFT already up, the Web add-in loaded and the test using it, navigate to **File |
Settings** and then open Internet Explorer. Now, navigate to the Google+ sign-in page.

2. At the bottom of the page, there is a list from which one can select a language;
select **Afrikaans**.

3. In UFT, navigate to **Resources | Object Repository...** (or use the *Ctrl + R* shortcut),
as shown in the following screenshot:

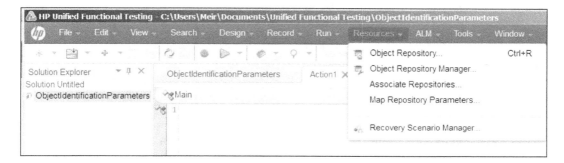

4. Click on the **+** icon bearing the tooltip **Add Objects to Local**, select the sign in button
with the mouse icon, and then add it to the OR.

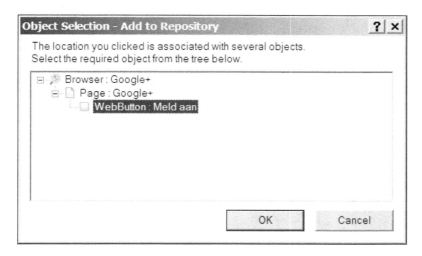

5. Click on the text to the right of the `name` property, and then click on the icon that appears to the right, as shown:

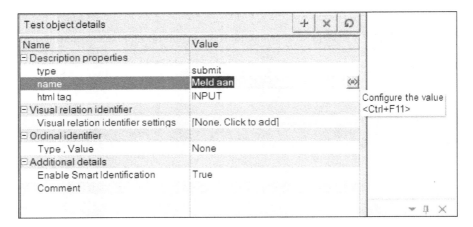

6. In the **Value Configuration Options** dialog that opens, select **Parameter**. Now, from the drop-down list in the **Parameter** field, select **Environment**, as shown in the following screenshot:

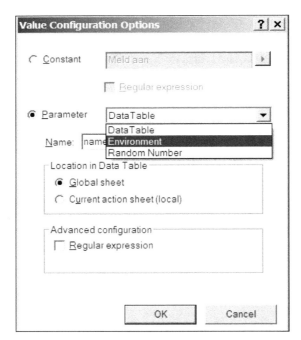

7. In the **name** field (combobox), type `<Google_Sign_In>`. Leave the value as is and click on **OK**.

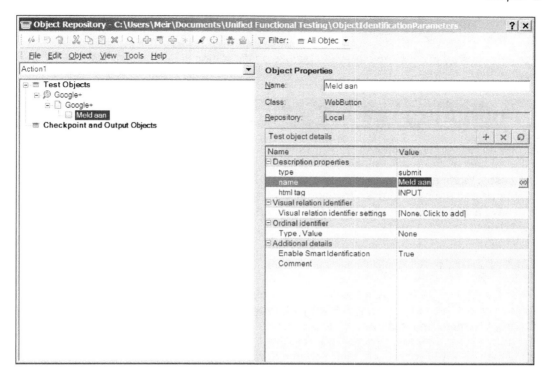

8. In OR, you will now notice that the value of the **name** property has changed to `<Google_Sign_in>` and the icon on the left represents the `Environment` object.

When running the test, OR will take the value of the **name** property from the Environment variable. Hence, if we have a set of such values for each language, then we will be able to test an application in whichever language we choose, without having to change a single line of script code!

 As with this method, the value is stored as an internal Environment variable, and we wish to load the values according to the language interface under test. We need to export the environment to an external XML file and load it at the beginning of the run session.

There's more...

The same basic approach can be used for object identification with the *Using Descriptive Programming inline* recipe of *Chapter 5, Object Identification*.

See also

The *Importing an Excel file to a test* and *Using a configuration file to manage test environments* recipes.

Defining test cases using a DataTable

As mentioned earlier, a data-driven test is one that is designed to behave as required by different sets of parameter values. Basically, such sets of values actually represent different test cases. When executing a login test action, for example, valid or invalid values for the username and the password will trigger different application responses. Of course, the best is to have a single action (or function) that will handle all cases, with the flow branching according to the input data.

Getting ready

Ensure that you have the Flight Reservation sample application shipped with the installed UFT. You can check this by navigating to **Start** | **All Programs** | **HP Software** | **Unified Functional Testing** | **Sample Applications**. You should have a shortcut named **Flight GUI** that launches `flight4a.exe`. Create a new test by navigating to **File** | **New** | **Test** from the menu, or by using the *Ctrl + N* keyboard shortcut. Rename `Action1` to `FR_Login` (optional).

How to do it...

Proceed with the following steps:

1. In the DataTable, select the `FR_Login` (or `Action1` if you decided not to rename it) datasheet. Create the following parameters in the DataTable (as described in the *Creating a DataTable parameter* recipe):

    - ❑ `TC_ID`
    - ❑ `Agent`
    - ❑ `Password`
    - ❑ `Button`
    - ❑ `Message1`
    - ❑ `Message2`
    - ❑ `Description`

2. We will derive the test cases with reference to the system requirements, as we know (for this example, we will ignore the **Cancel** and **Help** buttons):

   ❏ The correct login password is always `mercury`. A wrong password triggers an appropriate message.

   ❏ The agent name must be at least four characters long. If shorter, the application prompts the user with an appropriate message.

   ❏ An empty agent name triggers an appropriate message.

   ❏ An empty password triggers an appropriate message.

   ❏ After four consecutive failed login attempts with a wrong password, the application prompts the user with an appropriate message and then closes.

   Accordingly, we will enter the following data to represent the test cases:

#	TC_ID	Agent	Password	Button	Message1	Message2	Description
1	AgentEmpty		mercury	**OK**	Please enter agent name		Empty agent
2	AgentLT4	Mer	mercury	**OK**	Agent name must be at least 4 characters long		Agent with less than 4 characters
3	Agent4EmptyPass	Merc		**OK**	Please enter password		Wrong password #1 (empty)
4	Agent4WrongPass	Merc	Merc	**OK**	Incorrect password. Please try again		Wrong password #2
5	Agent4WrongPass	Merc	1234	**OK**	Incorrect password. Please try again		Wrong password #3
6	Agent4WrongPass	Merc	Gfrgfgh	**OK**	Incorrect password. Please try again	Login unsuccessful. Please try again later.	Wrong password #4; App closes
7	SuccessfulLogin	mercury	mercury	**OK**			Correct username and password

3. Apart from learning the TOs for the login and the message dialogs, create two checkpoints for the messages that appear after unsuccessful logins (one for the first and the other for the second type mentioned in the preceding table), and name them `Message1` and `Message2` respectively.

OR should contain the following TOs (smart identification should be turned off):

- ❏ `Dialog`: Login (`parent: none, description: text=Login, nativeclass=#32770, is owned window=False, is child window=False`)

- ❏ `WinEdit`: Agent Name (`parent: Dialog Login, description: nativeclass=Edit, attached text=Agent Name:`)

- ❏ `WinEdit`: Password (`parent: Dialog Login, description: nativeclass=Edit, attached text=Password:`)

- ❏ `WinButton`: OK (`parent: Dialog Login, description: text=OK, nativeclass=Button`)

- ❏ `Dialog`: Flight Reservations (`parent: Dialog Login, description: text= Flight Reservations, nativeclass=#32770, is owned window=True, is child window=False`)

- ❏ `Static`: Message (`parent: Dialog Flight Reservations, description: window id=65535, nativeclass=Static`)

- ❏ `WinButton`: OK (`parent: Dialog Flight Reservations, description: text=OK, nativeclass=Button`)

- ❏ `Window`: Flight Reservation (`parent: none, description: regexpwndtitle=Flight Reservation, regexpwndclas=Afx:, is owned window=False, is child window=False`)

- ❏ `WinButton`: Delete Order (`parent: Window Flight Reservation, description: text=&Delete Order, nativeclass=Button`)

- ❏ `WinButton`: Insert Order (`parent: Window Flight Reservation, description: text=&Insert Order, nativeclass=Button`)

- ❏ `WinButton`: Update Order (`parent: Window Flight Reservation, description: text=&Update Order, nativeclass=Button`)

- ❏ `WinButton`: FLIGHT (`parent: Window Flight Reservation, description: text=FLIGHT, nativeclass=Button`)

- ❏ `WinRadioButton`: First (`parent: Window Flight Reservation, description: text=First, nativeclass=Button`)

OR should contain the following `Checkpoint` objects:

- ❏ `Message1` and `Message2`: These checkpoints identify the static text appearing in the message that opens after a failed attempt to log in. The checkpoints should verify the `enabled=True` and `text=LocalSheet` DataTable parameters for `Message1` and `Message2` respectively.

- ❏ `Flight Reservation`: This checkpoint verifies that the main window opens with the properties `enabled=True` and with `text (title)=Flight Reservation`.

- ❏ `Delete Order`, `Insert Order`, and `Update Order`: All three checkpoints should verify that the buttons have the `enabled=False` and `text` properties set while opening the main application window set as their learned text property with the ampersand character (&) in the beginning of the string.

- ❏ `First`: This checkpoint for the `WinRadiobutton` should verify that upon opening the main application window, the properties `enabled=False` and `checked=OFF` are set.

4. In `FR_Login (Action1)`, write the following code:

```
'Checks if either the Login or the Main window is already
  open
Function appNotOpen()
    appNotOpen = true
    If Dialog("Login").Exist(0) or Window("Flight
      Reservation").Exist(0) Then
        appNotOpen = false
    End If
End Function


'Opens the application if not already open
Function openApp()
    If appNotOpen() Then
        SystemUtil.Run "C:\Program Files\HP\Unified
          Functional Testing\samples\flight\
          app\flight4a.exe","","C:\Program Files\HP\Unified
          Functional Testing\samples\flight\app\",""
        openApp = Dialog("Login").WaitProperty("enabled",
          1, 5000)
    else
```

```
            openApp = true
        End If
    End function


    'Handles the Login dialog: Enters the Agent Name and the
      Password and clicks on the OK button
    Function login(agentName, password, button)
        with Dialog("Login")
            .WinEdit("Agent Name").Set agentName
            .WinEdit("Password").SetSecure password
            .WinButton(button).Click
            If .exist(0) Then
                login = false
            else
                login = true
            End If
        end with
    End Function


    'Performs a standard checkpoint on a message open by the FR
      application
    Function checkMessage(id)
        If Dialog("Login").Dialog("Flight
          Reservations").Exist(0) Then
            checkMessage = Dialog("Login").Dialog("Flight
              Reservations").Static("Message").Check(CheckPoint
              ("Message"&id))
            Dialog("Login").Dialog("Flight
              Reservations").WinButton("OK").Click
        else
            checkMessage = false
        End if
    End Function


    'Performs several standard checkpoints on the Main window
      and on several of its child objects
    'to verify its initial state
    function verifyMainWndInitialState()
        with Window("Flight Reservation")
            if .Check(CheckPoint("Flight Reservation")) then
                .WinButton("FLIGHT").Check CheckPoint("FLIGHT")
                .WinRadioButton("First").Check
                  CheckPoint("First")
```

```
                .WinButton("Update Order").Check
                  CheckPoint("Update Order")
                .WinButton("Delete Order").Check
                  CheckPoint("Delete Order")
                .WinButton("Insert Order").Check
                  CheckPoint("Insert Order")
            End if
        end with
End function

'Variables declaration and initialization
Dim agentName, password, button

agentName = DataTable("AgentName", dtLocalSheet)
password = DataTable("Password", dtLocalSheet)
button = DataTable("Button", dtLocalSheet)

'Tries to open the application
If not openApp() Then
    ExitTest
End If

'Tries to login with the input data
if not login(agentName, password, button) Then
    'Checks if a warning/error message opened, if it's
      correct in context and closes it
    if checkMessage("1") then
        'Checks if a second warning/error message opened,
          if it's correct in context and closes it
        if checkMessage("2") then
            If not Dialog("Login").Exist(0) Then
                reporter.ReportEvent micPass, "Login",
                  "Maximum number of trials exceeded.
                  Application closed."
                'If a second message opened, then the
                  number of login trials was exceeded and
                  the application closed, so we need to
                  reopen the application
                call openApp()
            End If
        End if
    End If
else
    call verifyMainWndInitialState()
End if 'Tries to login
```

How it works...

Now, we will explain the flow of the `FR_Login` action and the local functions.

We declare the variables that we need for the `Login` operation, namely, `AgentName`, `Password`, and `Button`. We then initialize them by retrieving their values from the local sheet in the DataTable. The `button` value is parameterized to enable further elaboration of the code to incorporate the cases of clicking on the `Cancel` and `Help` buttons.

Next, we call the `openApp()` function and check the returned value. If it is `False`, then the Flight Reservation application did not open, and therefore we exit the test.

We attempt to log in and pass the `AgentName`, `Password`, and `Button` parameters to the function. If it returns `true`, then login was successful and the `else` block of code is executed where we call the `verifyMainWndInitialState()` function to assert that the main window opened as expected.

If the login did not succeed, we check the first message with a checkpoint that compares the actual text with the text recorded in the DataTable, which is correct in the context of the planned flow.

If the first message check passes, then we check to see if there is another message. Of course, we could have used a counter for the actual password failures to see if the second message is shown exactly by the fourth attempt. However, as we set the input data, the flow is planned such that it must appear at the right time. This is the true sense of defining test cases with input data. If a message appears, then the `checkMessage(id)` function closes the message box. We then check if the login dialog box is closed with the code `If not Dialog("Login").Exist(0) Then`, and it then calls `openApp()` to begin again for the last iteration.

In the last iteration, with the input data on the seventh row (refer to the table in the previous section), the script performs a successful login, and then calls the function `verifyMainWndInitialState()`, as mentioned in the previous section.

Storing data in the Environment object

The `Environment` global object is one of UFT's reserved objects and it can be used to store and retrieve both runtime and design-time data.

> For a more detailed description of the `Environment` object, please see the next recipe *Retrieving data from the Environment object*.

How to do it...

Proceed with the following steps:

1. To store a parameter at design time, navigate to **File | Settings** from the UFT menu and then select **Environment**. From the **Variable type** list box, select **User-defined**, as shown in the following screenshot:

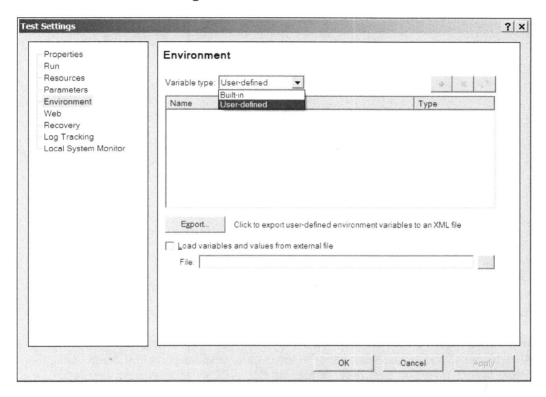

2. Click on the **+** button on the right of your **Environment** window. The **Add New Environment Parameter** window will open. Enter the new parameter's (variable) name and value:

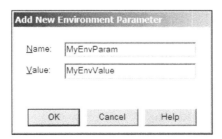

3. Click on the **OK** button to approve. You will notice that the newly created variable, with its value, now appears on the list. You should pay attention to the **Type** column, in which it indicates that the variable we just created is `Internal`:

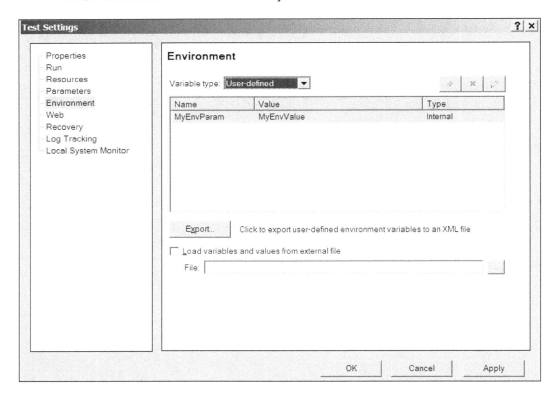

What does it mean? A user-defined variable is `Internal` when we define it through the UFT GUI. It becomes `External` when either we export the variables to an XML file or define them directly in such a file and later, load the file with the variables and values to the test.

How it works...

Definitions of the types of variable classifications are as follows:

> ► **Internal variables**: When you open an existing test, which has an `Internal` variable defined, these will be loaded automatically. Changes made to their values during the run session will not be saved. In this sense, the values given to `Internal` variables using the GUI can be referred to as default values.

> ► **External variables**: When you open an existing test, which has its user-defined variables loaded from an external XML file, these will be loaded automatically. Their values cannot be changed during the run session. In this sense, the values given to `External` variables can be referred to as constant values.

There's more...

We can also store a value to an Environment variable dynamically from the code. Such a variable will have global scope but will be accessible during runtime only. This means that you will not see it in the list of `Internal` variables, as shown in this recipe. The procedure is equivalent to using the default `Add` method of the `Scripting.Dictionary` object, as shown in the following line of code:

```
Environment("MyEnvParam") = "MyEnvValue"
```

See also

Refer to an article by Yaron Assa at `http://www.advancedqtp.com/reserved-objects-as-an-env-object-replacement`.

Retrieving data from the Environment object

This recipe will show you how to retrieve data from the `Environment` object, which is a kind of dictionary that stores key-value pairs. As we will see, unlike a regular dictionary, the `Environment` object stores two types of variables:

▸ Built-in
▸ User-defined

Built-in Environment variables give access to two types of information:

▸ **Static data** such as the `OS`, `OSVersion`, `LocalHostName`, `SystemTempDir`, `ProductDir` (where UFT is installed), `ProductName`, `ProductVer` (UFT version), `UserName` (the Windows login name), and several settings such as `UpdatingCheckpoints` and `UpdatingTODescriptions`. In addition, we can retrieve information about the current test, such as `TestName` and `TestDir` (the path to the current test(s) from the `Environment` object).

▸ **Runtime data** such as `TestIteration`, `ActionName`, and `ActionIteration` can be retrieved via the `Environment` object during runtime. The iteration number can be useful, for instance, when we need to perform an initialization procedure that should be done only once. In this case, the iteration number must be equal to the `TestIteration` parameter value.

Getting ready

Create a user-defined Environment variable named `MyEnvParam` (see the previous recipe, *Storing data in the Environment object*).

How to do it...

The following code shows how to retrieve either a built-in or a user-defined variable:

```
Print Environment("TestDir")
'Prints the Built-in TestDir (path) Environment variable to the
console
Print Environment("MyEnvParam")
'Prints the User-defined MyEnvParam Environment variable to the
console
```

How it works...

Similar to the workings of the `Scripting.Dictionary` object, by accessing an existing key, the `Environment` object returns its paired value.

See also

User-defined Environment variables can be stored in an XML file and dynamically loaded during the runtime session. Refer to the *Using global variables (Environment)* recipe of *Chapter 8, Utility and Reserved Objects*.

Reading values from an INI file

Files with the extension `.ini` are the legacy of the old Windows versions (16 bit). In the past, they were extensively used—and still are to some extent—ubiquitously to store the settings for applications. Nowadays, it is common practice to store settings in the registry. Though textual, such files have a very well-defined structure; there are sections and key-value pairs. A section starts with a label enclosed in square brackets: `[section-name]` and a key-value is implemented as `<variable name>=<value>`. Such a structure could be useful, for instance, if we wanted to keep the settings organized by environments or by user profiles within an `.ini` file.

In this recipe, you will also see an example of how to use the `Extern` reserved object to define references to methods in external DLLs, such as those of the Win32API. These methods can then be loaded and executed during runtime. A more elaborate description is available in the *Drawing a rectangle on the screen with Win32 API methods (Extern)* recipe of *Chapter 8, Utility and Reserved Objects*.

Getting ready

To complete this recipe, we need to use the global `Extern` object, which with proper use provides the UFT with access to the methods of an external **Dynamic Link Library** (**DLL**). We will define a variable and assign it a reference to the global `Extern` object (this is done to avoid persistence, as `Extern` is a reserved object not released from memory until UFT closes):

```
Dim oExtern
set oExtern = Extern
```

Then, we will declare the method or methods we wish to call from the relevant Win32API. In this case, the method is `GetPrivateProfileString`, which retrieves the value of a given key within a specific section:

```
oExtern.Declare micInteger,"GetPrivateProfileString",
    "kernel32.dll","GetPrivateProfileStringA", _
            micString, micString, micString,
                micString+micByRef, micInteger, micString
```

How to do it...

After defining the connection to the DLL with its returned value and arguments, we can retrieve the value of any key within a given section. In the following example, the `ConfigFileVersion` key specified in the file `wrls.ini` is located in the `UFT/bin` folder. In the end, the `Extern` object reference is destroyed at the end of the run:

```
call oExtern.GetPrivateProfileString("ProgramInformation",
    "ConfigFileVersion", "", RetVal, 255, "C:\Program
    Files\HP\Unified Functional Testing\bin\wrls_ins.ini")
print  RetVal

set oExtern = nothing
```

The output to the console in this case was the string `1.05`.

Using a configuration file to manage test environments

As shown in the previous recipe, it is possible to read variable values from an `.ini` file. We will show how to define several environments within such a file and load the input data for the current environment during runtime.

Getting ready

Follow the same steps stated in the *Getting ready* section of the *Reading values from an INI file* recipe.

How to do it...

Create a new file with the name `QA-env-settings.ini`. Enter the following entries to create three sets of parameters corresponding to three test environments QA1, QA2, and QA3:

```
[QA1]
InputDataSrc= "RegressionData1.xls"
Username       = "user1"
URL            = "http://www.url1.com"
Description = "Data for QA1 environment"

[QA2]
InputDataSrc= "RegressionData2.xls"
Username       = "user2"
URL            = "http://www.url2.com"
Description = "Data for QA2 environment"

[QA3]
InputDataSrc = "RegressionData3.xls"
Username       = "user3"
URL            = "http://www.url3.com"
Description = "Data for QA3 environment"
```

In our test, we will load the input data based on the value of the Environment variable QA_ENV, which will take one of the following environments: QA1, QA2, or QA3. Before running the test, ensure that the variable exists, and provide the value for the required testing environment (see the *Storing data in the Environment object* recipe). Therefore, our code in `Action1` will look like the following code snippet:

```
Dim sDataSourcePath, sURL, sUsername

oExtern.GetPrivateProfileString(Environment("QA_ENV"), _
```

```
"InputDataSrc", "", sDataSourcePath, 255, _
"QA_env_settings.ini")

oExtern.GetPrivateProfileString(Environment("QA_ENV"), _
"InputDataSrc", "", sURL, 255, "QA_env_settings.ini")

oExtern.GetPrivateProfileString(Environment("QA_ENV"), _
"InputDataSrc", "", sUsername, 255, "QA_env_settings.ini")

DataTable.Import(sDataSourcePath)
```

How it works...

We retrieve the value of the `QA_ENV` Environment variable, and accordingly load the values of the variables in the corresponding section in the `.ini` file. The value of the `InputDataSrc` key within the corresponding section is then retrieved (note that the parameter is passed by reference and filled by the target method) and is used to import the Excel file (as you can see in the *Importing an Excel file to a test* recipe) that contains the input data for the given testing environment.

Using a global dictionary for fast shared data access

Using a DataTable is a generally good practice because spreadsheet data is easy to create, visualize, and maintain. This is because MS Excel lies behind the `DataTable`, which is, as mentioned before, a wrapper to the Excel COM object. Other advantages of using the `DataTable` include its full integration with the test and action iterations mechanism and with the results report, in which one can visualize each iteration, along with the input data.

This is all good for the retrieval of input data that is prepared during design time. However, using the `DataTable` for sharing between actions has two main drawbacks during runtime:

- Repeated writes and reads may hinder performance when it comes to a large number of iterations and a large number of parameters, as is quite often the case with many information systems.

- Sharing data with `GlobalSheet` is very difficult to implement. For example, suppose we need to store the `CustomerID` given by the system upon customer creation. In `GlobalSheet`, it will be stored at the current row. Though we may set the exact row using the `DataTable` method, that is, `SetCurrentRow (<rownumber>)`, it is still a question of how to ensure that at a later stage, an action that needs a `CustomerID` would know the correct row number.

An alternative to sharing data among actions would be to use the UFT's built-in `Output` and `Input` parameters. However, `Input` parameters are good only to pass data from an action to its nested (called) actions, and `Output` parameters are good only to pass data to other sibling actions (that is, those which are at the same hierarchical level). Hence, they do not enable the flexibility one may need when testing complex systems and are cumbersome to manage.

A better approach is to have the data that must be shared and stored in the `Dictionary` object of a global scope. A `Dictionary` object is actually a hash table with a capacity to store values of different types, such as strings, numbers, Booleans, arrays, and references to objects (including other nested `Dictionary` objects, which is a powerful, yet very advanced technique that is out of scope here). Each value is stored with a unique key by which it can be accessed later.

Getting ready

In UFT, create a new function library by navigating to **File | New | Function Library** (or use the key shortcut *Alt + Shift + N*) and save it as `UFT_Globals.vbs`. It is recommended to save it in a folder, which would be shared later by all tests.

Navigate to **File | Settings** and attach the function library to the test.

How to do it...

As any public variable declared in a function library attached to a test can be accessed by any action, we will define a global variable and two functions to initialize `initGlobalDictionary` and dispose `disposeGlobalDictionary`:

```
Dim GlobalDictionary

Function initGlobalDictionary()
    If not (lcase(typename(GlobalDictionary)) = "dictionary") Then
        Set GlobalDictionary =
            CreateObject("Scripting.Dictionary")
    End If
End Function
Function disposeGlobalDictionary()
    Set GlobalDictionary = nothing
End Function
```

The initGlobalDictionary() function will check if the public variable GlobalDictionary was not initialized earlier, and then set it with a reference to a new instance of a Dictionary object, as mentioned in the previous code. The disposeGlobalDictionary() function is given for the sake of completeness, as in any case, memory is released when the test stops. However, we may wish to empty the GlobalDictionary variable in certain cases, so it is recommended to include this function as well.

Now, in Action1 (or whichever action runs first in our test), we will write the following code:

```
If cint(Environment("TestIteration")) = 1 and
   cint(Environment("ActionIteration")) = 1 Then
      call initGlobalDictionary()
End If
```

The previous code will ensure that the GlobalDictionary variable is instantiated only once at the beginning of the run session. If we need a new instance for every test iteration, then we just need to change the code to the following lines of code, so that we get a new instance only at the start of the first Action1 iteration:

```
If CInt(Environment("ActionIteration")) = 1 Then
      call initGlobalDictionary()
End If
```

With our test set up this way, we can now use this global object to share data as in the following example. Create a new Action2 DataTable and make it run after Action1 (at the end of the test). Now, write the following code in Action1:

```
GlobalDictionary.Add "CustomerID", "123456789"
Print Environment("ActionName") & ": " &
   GlobalDictionary("CustomerID")
```

In Action2, write the following code:

```
Print Environment("ActionName") & ": " &
   GlobalDictionary("CustomerID")
```

It is strongly recommended to remove a key from the dictionary when it is no longer required:

```
GlobalDictionary.Remove "CustomerID"
```

Alternatively, to remove all keys from the dictionary altogether at the end of a test iteration or at the beginning of a test iteration greater than the first, use the following line of code:

```
GlobalDictionary.RemoveAll
```

As mentioned earlier, keys must be unique and if we use the same keys in each test iteration, it would cause a runtime error with the first key found to exist in the dictionary. Another way, as mentioned earlier, is to call the `disposeGlobalDictionary` at the end of each test iteration and the `initializeGlobalDictionary()` method at the start.

How it works...

When you run this test, in `Action1`, it first creates a new `Dictionary` instance and assigns a reference to the public variable `GlobalDictionary`. Then, it adds a new key `CustomerID` with the value `123456789`, and prints the action name from the Environment built-in runtime variables ("`Action1`") and the value, by referring to the `CustomerID` key we just added. Then, it executes `Action2`, where it again prints in the same manner as in `Action1`. However, as the `ActionName` Environment variable is dynamic, it prints "`Action2`". This is to prove that `Action2` actually has access to the key and value added in `Action1`. The output of this test is as shown in the screenshot:

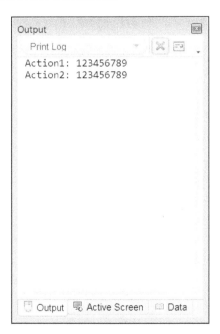

See also

Refer to the *Using a global dictionary for fast shared code access* recipe.

Using a global dictionary for fast shared code access

As we have shown in the recipe *Using a global dictionary for fast shared data access*, it is possible to use a dictionary to store values of different types during runtime, and share them during the test flow with other actions at any level. We mentioned that a dictionary has the capacity to store any type of value, including objects. We further indicated that this opens the possibility to have nested dictionaries (albeit out of the scope of the current chapter).

In a similar fashion, it is possible to load pieces of code globally and hence grant shared access to all actions. In order to achieve this, we will recur to a well-known code design pattern, the command wrapper.

Getting ready

Refer to the *Getting ready* section of the *Using a global dictionary for fast shared data access* recipe. Basically, we can just add the code to the same function library and actions.

How to do it...

The first steps of defining the `GlobalDictionary` variable and the functions to manage its instantiation and disposal are identical, as in the recipe *Using a global dictionary for fast shared data access*, so we can just skip to the next step.

The remaining implementation deserves special attention. In the `Globals.vbs` function library that we attached to the test, we will add the following pieces of code:

```
Class MyOperation1
    Function Run()
        Print typename(me) & " is now running..."
    End Function
End Class

Class MyOperation2
    Function Run()
        Print typename(me) & " is now running..."
    End Function
End Class

Function GetInstance(cls)
    Dim obj

    On error resume next
    Execute "set obj = new " & cls
```

```
        If err.number <> 0 Then
            reporter.ReportEvent micFail, "GetInstance", "Class " &
            cls & " is not defined (error #" & err.number & ")"
            Set obj = nothing
        End If
        Set GetInstance = obj
    End Function
```

The two classes follow the command wrapper design pattern. Note that they both contain a `Run` function (any name would do). This follows a pattern, which enables us to load an instance of each class and store it in our `GlobalDictionary` variable.

The `GetInstance(cls)` function acts as a generic constructor for our encapsulated functions. It is absolutely necessary to have such a constructor in the function library because UFT does not support instantiating classes with the operator `new` within an action. We use the `Execute` function to make the line of code, resulting from concatenating the command string with the `cls` parameter passed to the function, and hence, it can return an instance of any class contained in any other associated function library. The function checks if an error occurs while trying to create a new instance of the given class. This could happen if the string naming the class is inaccurate. In such a case, the function returns nothing after reporting a failure to the test report. In such a case, we may wish to halt the test run altogether by using the `ExitTest` command.

In `Action1`, we will add the following code:

```
GlobalDictionary.Add "Op1", GetInstance("MyOperation1")
GlobalDictionary.Add "Op2", GetInstance("MyOperation2")
```

In `Action2`, we will add the following code:

```
GlobalDictionary("Op1").Run
GlobalDictionary("Op2").Run
```

The output of the test is now as shown in the following screenshot:

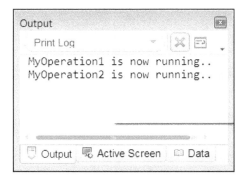

How it works...

When you run this test, the initial process of `GlobalDictionary` instantiation is executed, as in the previous recipe. Then, we simply add two keys to the `GlobalDictionary` and assign a reference to each value to an instance of the command wrapper classes `MyOperation1` and `MyOperation2`. When the test flow reaches `Action2`, we access these instances by retrieving the items (or the values) we stored with the keys, and then have access to the classes' public methods, fields, and properties. The code line is as follows:

```
GlobalDictionary("Op1").Run
```

First, it retrieves the reference to the `MyOperation1` object, and then, it applies to the `Op1` operator to access the public `Run` method, which just prints the name of the class and a string.

There's more...

Of course, the `Run` method of the command wrapper pattern may need a variable number of arguments, because different functions meet different requirements. This can easily be resolved by defining the `Run` method as accepting one argument and passing a `Dictionary` object with the keys and values for each variable that is required.

For example, assuming that the `dic` argument is a dictionary:

```
Class MyOperation1
    Function Run(dic)
        Print typename(me) & " is now running..."
        Print dic("var1")
        Print dic("var2")
        Print typename(me) & " ended running..."
    End Function
End Class
```

Now, we would use the following code in `Action2` to call the `Run` method:

```
Set dic = CreateObject("Scripting.Dictionary")
dic.Add "var1", "Some value"
dic.Add "var2", "Some other value"
GlobalDictionary("Op1").Run
```

See also

Also refer to the *Using a global dictionary for fast shared data access* recipe in this chapter. We will also delve more in depth into the command wrapper design pattern in *Chapter 7, Using Classes*.

2
Testing Web Pages

In this chapter, we will cover:

- ▸ Checking whether page links are broken
- ▸ Deleting cookies
- ▸ Managing multiple browser windows
- ▸ Handling pop-up dialogs
- ▸ Downloading a file using XMLHttp
- ▸ Checking whether a website is up
- ▸ Uploading a file using FTP
- ▸ Identifying elements based on anchors
- ▸ Synchronizing a test with a web page loading
- ▸ Accessing web elements through DOM

Introduction

Unlike desktop (client) applications, the Web poses specific challenges that go beyond the local machine. For instance, a web page may not display the intended content correctly with regard to content, format, layout, and even functionality, due to missing or corrupted resources located on a remote server. An application server, a database server, a **Cascading Style Sheet** (**CSS**), and a configuration or JavaScript file (.js) are among the resources that may have an impact on the web application functioning. Other challenges include the integrity of the links, JavaScript bugs, and caching effects, to name a few. Security issues may also prevent web pages from displaying contents properly, as is the case with images loaded across domains.

Automating tests for the GUI of a web page poses challenges related to script page synchronization, object identification, and checking dynamic content, among others. This chapter describes various common automation tasks related to the testing of web pages.

 This chapter is not intended to be a tutorial on web technology, so some basic background is required, for instance, being acquainted with basic concepts such as **Document Object Model** (**DOM**). To learn about DOM, it is recommended that you refer to the official specification at http://www.w3.org/TR/DOM-Level-3-Core/introduction.html.

Checking whether page links are broken

Links are the most essential elements on a web page, as they are the connection between different sections on a page, other pages, and external pages. A link must lead to a valid **Uniform Resource Locator** (**URL**). If it leads to a non-existing or otherwise unavailable page, then it will be marked as broken.

A link that is a permanent element of a page is also called a permalink. Such a link is expected to always appear on a web page, and it will always lead to the same URL. Such a link is easy to map, either with OR, or using descriptive programming. However, in many web applications, links lead to dynamically generated pages, such as customer information, search results, and so on. Needless to say, their `href` attribute is also dynamically built, based on data that is known only during runtime. On a search results page, such as those generated by Google and other search engines, even the number of links may vary. This is also true for billing information and call details pages, which the web interface of mobile operators displays to customers.

Testing links is one of the very basic tasks that automation can tackle very efficiently, and hence, you need to free the manual tester to perform other tasks. In this recipe, we will see a very simple method to check that links on a page are not broken.

Getting ready

From the **File** menu on the UFT home page, navigate to **New** | **Function Library**, or use the *Alt* + *Shift* + *N* shortcut. Name the new function library as `Web_Functions.vbs`.

How to do it...

The seemingly obvious approach would be to get the collection of links on the page first, and then retrieve the value of the `href` attribute for each link and click on the `href` value. After the target page loads, check the URL and compare it to the original value taken from `href`. Basically, this is more or less what a manual tester would do. However, this process does not only check if a link is broken, but also checks if it is valid. This process is quite tedious and does not take into account the fact that in many cases, the value of `href` does not predict what would be the target URL. For example, the widespread usage of TinyURL!™ and redirections makes this approach impractical. Another complication is that some links load the target page on the same window and even the same tab, while others do it in a separate tab or window. While using a link is an essential part of the business flow, it is logical to actually open the new page (or navigate to the page on a new tab/window). After the target page loads, the test script can manipulate its elements and hence, continue the test flow as planned.

If, however, we just need to check that the links are not broken, then it is possible to do it using an instance of `MSXML2.XmlHttp`. In the following example, we will declare a global variable for this object and write four functions in `Web_RegisteredFunctions.vbs`:

- `DisposeXMLHttp()`: This function removes the reference to the global `oXMLHttp` variable
- `InitXMLHttp()`: This function creates an instance of `XMLHttp`, and then sets a reference to `oXMLHttp`
- `GetLinks(URL)`: This function retrieves all the links on a web page using a `Description` object
- `CheckLink(strHref)`: This function checks if a given link is broken or not

The code is as follows:

```
Dim oXMLHttp

Function disposeXMLHttp()
    Set oXMLHttp = Nothing
End Function
```

```
Function initXMLHttp()
    Set oXMLHttp = CreateObject("MSXML2.XmlHttp")
End Function

function getLinks(oPage)
    Dim oAllLinks, oDesc

    Set oDesc = Description.Create
    oDesc("html tag").value = "a|A"
    oDesc("html tag").regularexpression = true
    Set oAllLinks = oPage.ChildObjects(oDesc)

    set getLinks = oAllLinks
End function

Function checkLink(URL)
    If lcase(typename(oXMLHttp)) <> "xmlhttp" Then
        initXMLHttp()
    End If

    if oXMLHttp.open("GET", URL, false) = 0 then
        On error resume next
        oXMLHttp.send()

        If oXMLHttp.Status<>200 Then
            reporter.ReportEvent micFail, "Check Link", "Link " &
                URL & " is broken: " & oXMLHttp.Status
        Else
            reporter.ReportEvent micPass, "Check Link", "Link " &
                URL & " is OK"
        End If
    End if
End Function
```

We then run `Action1` with the following lines of code:

```
Dim i, j, oPage, oAllLinks, regex, sHref

call initXMLHttp()
'We build a filter to exclude links that are not "real", direct
  links but email, section and share links,
```

```
Set regex = new RegExp
regex.pattern = "mailto:|\#|share=(facebook|google\-
    plus|linkedin|twitter|email)"
regex.ignorecase = true
regex.global = true

Set oPage = Browser("name:=.+").Page("title:=.+")

j=0
set oAllLinks = getLinks(oPage)
print "Total number of links: " & oAllLinks.count
For i = 0 to oAllLinks.count-1
    If oAllLinks(i).Exist(0) Then
        On error resume next
        sHref=oAllLinks(i).Object.href

        If not regex.test(sHref) Then
            j=j+1
            print j & ": " & sHref
            call checkLink(sHref)
        else
            reporter.ReportNote i & " - " & sHref & " is a mailto,
                section or share link."
        End if
        If err.number <> 0 Then
            reporter.ReportEvent micWarning, "Check Link", "Error:
                " & err.number & " - Description: " &
                err.description
        End If
        On error goto 0
    else
        reporter.ReportEvent micWarning, "Check Link",
            oAllLinks(i).GetTOProperty("href") & " does not exist."
    End If
Next
print "Total number of processed links: " & j

disposeXMLHttp()
```

How it works...

In the function library, we declared `objXMLHttp` as a variable of global scope. The `InitXMLHttp()` and `DisposeXMLHttp()` functions take care of creating and disposing the instance of the `MSXML2.XmlHttp` class. The `GetLinks(objPage)` function uses a `Description` object to retrieve the collection of all links from a page with a regular expression (HTML a or A tag). This collection is returned by the `GetLinks(objPage)` function to the calling action, where, for each item (link) in the collection, it retrieves and passes the `href` attribute to the `CheckLink(strHref)` function. The latter method checks the link by opening a connection to the URL given by `strHref` and waiting for a HTTP response to the `send` command. If the target URL is available, then the status of the HTTP response should be `200`. We also check if there is some error during the process, with `On Error Resume Next` as a precaution. (It is important to keep in mind that this may not work together with UFT's out-of-the-box settings for error handling, by navigating to **Test** | **Settings** | **Run**. This will work perfectly; using this setting, proceed to the next step). This is done because sometimes, a link that is retrieved at the start of the process may not be available when we actually wish to execute the checkpoint, as is the case with sliders and galleries with changing content.

There's more...

It is possible to further analyze the returned status with a `Select Case` decision structure to report exactly what the problem is (**404=Page not found, 500=Internal Server Error**, and so on).

See also

For technical documentation of the `open` method of the `XMLHTTPRequest` object used in this recipe, please refer to `http://msdn.microsoft.com/en-us/library/windows/desktop/ms757849(v=vs.85).aspx`.

Deleting cookies

Cookies are actually files containing data that is used by websites to remember user preferences and other relevant information, such as authentication credentials. In some cases, we may need to delete these cookies in order to do the following:

- Test if a site detects that the cookies are missing
- Test if a site responds according to the browser's configuration (for example, it prompts for approval, and then stores the selection)
- Test if a site responds according to the application requirements (for example, prompts for login if an authentication cookie is missing)

There are several ways to achieve deletion of cookies, but here we will show the simplest way with the undocumented `WebUtil` object and methods.

Getting ready

Let's take an example. From the **File** menu, navigate to **New | Test**, use the *Ctrl + N* shortcut, or use the `Web_Functions.vbs` library you created in the previous recipe, to encapsulate the commands in your own custom functions.

How to do it...

To delete all cookies, write the following code:

```
WebUtil.DeleteCookies()
```

To delete a specific cookie from a domain, write the following code:

```
WebUtil.DeleteCookie(Domain, Cookie)
```

To encapsulate the commands in custom functions, write the following functions in the function library:

```
Function DeleteCookies()
    WebUtil.DeleteCookies()
End Function
Function DeleteCookie(ByVal Domain, ByVal Cookie)
    WebUtil.DeleteCookie(Domain, Cookie)
End Function
```

The `WebUtil` object operates only with an **Internet Explorer** (**IE**) browser. To delete cookies for other browsers, a custom function needs to be programmed to find the correct folder in which these are stored and then perform their deletion.

How it works...

The previous code is self-evident. The first statement is equivalent to choosing to delete cookies through the IE **Internet Options** in the **Control Panel** window by navigating to **Browsing history** under the **General** tab, and then clicking on the **Delete...** button. This opens a **Delete Browsing History** dialog. The second statement deletes a specific cookie for a given domain. In that case, the name of the cookie must be accurate.

Managing multiple browser windows

In particular cases, we may face a requirement to handle multiple browser windows or tabs. A typical situation would be when clicking on a link or button, which leads to the opening of a page in a pop-up browser window, or in another tab within the same window. This new page might be a standard form, a Terms of Use page, or similar, and usually, this would either close automatically upon completing a data-filling process (as in the case of a form), after reading the document, or approving the terms, for instance. One of the challenges with dynamically created pages, which are generated on the fly, is that we do not wish to clutter our OR with such objects, but rather detect their presence during runtime, perform some checkpoints to verify if the content is correct, and proceed with the test flow (usually by closing the newly opened window first).

In other cases, we may need to test a complex web application with an administrator, client-side GUI and an end user client-side GUI. For instance, we might want to test how changes made by an administrator affect the way users use the application. A typical case would be, for example, one in which a power user makes policy changes and so restricts features to specific groups of users. Another related case example would be when a user needs to be banned. In such cases, one would like to perform some operations on the admin side, and test how they reflect on the end user side. To save time, we may wish to have both GUIs open in separate browser windows.

Getting ready

The suggested method involves using a global dictionary. For background on this topic, please refer to the *Using a global dictionary for fast shared data access* recipe in *Chapter 1, Data-driven Tests*, to learn how to define and use such a dictionary.

How to do it...

The general method to manage multiple browsers is to use an hWnd (window handle). First, we will get an hWnd for each browser window that opens and store it in a dedicated global dictionary that we will declare. Though it changes from one run session to another, the hWnd is always unique for an object, so it is the ultimate identifying property (though it is, of course, a chicken and egg problem, as you first need to identify the object using other properties). Yet, it is a good practice, especially because web applications quite often change the title of the page according to the current context. Basically, UFT identifies the object using the title. Other methods, such as `CreationTime`, are not robust enough, as `CreationTime` is a dynamic property that changes as browser windows open and close. The hWnd property, on the other hand, will remain constant as long as the browser window stays open.

So, while the browser window or tab is open, we will be able to refer to it through its associated key in the dictionary. When closing it, we shall remove the key-item pair from the dictionary. In such a way, we will be able to track the open browsers and access them using a key that reflects their function within the application context, without being sensitive to the content of the currently loaded page.

In the `Web_RegisteredFunctions.vbs` function library, put the following code:

```
Dim oBrowsers

Function initBrowsers()
    Set oBrowsers = CreateObject("scripting.dictionary")
End Function

Function disposeBrowsers()
    Set oBrowsers = nothing
End Function
```

This code will take care of initializing and disposing of the `objBrowsers` global variable.

In `Action1`, we will execute the following logic for each browser:

1. Open a browser window with a specified URL.
2. Identify the object using the `openurl` property, making sure the URL has opened. We will use a regular expression to suppress specific parameters that may be added automatically to the URL.
3. Retrieve the window handle (the `hWnd` property) and push it to `objBrowsers`.
4. Highlight each browser window by accessing the keys in `oBrowser`.
5. Close each browser window and remove each associated key.

The code is as follows:

```
Dim arrURL

initBrowsers()

arrURL = Array("advancedqtp.com", "taaas.net",
  "relevantcodes.com")

For i = 0 To ubound(arrURL)
    SystemUtil.Run "IExplore.exe", arrUrl(i)
    If Browser("openurl:=.*"&arrURL(i)&".*").Exist Then
        oBrowsers.Add arrURL(i), Browser("openurl:=.*"&arrURL
(i)&".*").GetROProperty("hwnd")
  else
```

```
            reporter.ReportEvent micFail, "Open Browser", "Browser
                didn't open with URL " & arrURL(i)
        End If
    Next

    'Show the Browsers
    For i = 0 To ubound(arrURL)
        print "hwnd:="&oBrowsers(arrURL(i))
        Browser("hwnd:="&oBrowsers(arrURL(i))).highlight
    Next

    'Close the Browsers
    For i = 0 To ubound(arrURL)
        print "Closing "& arrURL(i)
        Browser("hwnd:="&oBrowsers(arrURL(i))).close
        if not Browser("hwnd:="&oBrowsers(arrURL(i))).Exist(0) then
            oBrowsers.Remove arrURL(i)
            print oBrowsers.count
        End if
    Next

    disposeBrowsers()
```

A good alternative would be to actually add a reference to the `Browser` object itself. The rest of the logic remains the same. The code is as follows:

```
    Dim arrURL

    initBrowsers()

    arrURL = Array("advancedqtp.com", "taaas.net",
      "relevantcodes.com")

    For i = 0 To ubound(arrURL)
        SystemUtil.Run "IExplore.exe", arrUrl(i)
        If Browser("openurl:=.*"&arrURL(i)&".*").Exist Then
            oBrowsers.Add arrURL(i), Browser("openurl:=.*"&arrURL(i)&".*")
        else
            reporter.ReportEvent micFail, "Open Browser", "Browser
                didn't open with URL " & arrURL(i)
        End If
    Next
```

```
'Show the Browsers
For i = 0 To ubound(arrURL)
    oBrowsers(arrURL(i)).highlight
Next

'Close the Browsers
For i = 0 To ubound(arrURL)
    print "Closing "& arrURL(i)
    oBrowsers(arrURL(i)).close
    if not oBrowsers(arrURL(i)).Exist(0) then
        oBrowsers.Remove arrURL(i)
        print oBrowsers.count
    End if
Next

disposeBrowsers()
```

How it works...

First, we initialize the `objBrowsers` global object, which is actually a dictionary. Next, we open three browser windows using `SystemUtil.Run`, invoking `IExplore.exe` (Internet Explorer's executable) for each URL, as defined in our `arrURL` array variable. For each browser that opens, we store a key with the URL and either assign it `hWnd` or a reference to a `Browser` TO. We then traverse the items in `objBrowsers` with the keys, access each TO using descriptive programming with `Browser("hwnd:="&objBrowsers(arrURL(i)))`, and highlight them to demonstrate the correct identification. Finally, we close each browser using its `objBrowsers` key, and after verifying that it is closed, we remove the key from `objBrowsers` to keep our list updated.

Handling pop-up dialogs

It is common to encounter pop-up dialogs that open up while using software applications. Mostly, these are application modals, which mean that no further operations can be performed within the application context until the dialog is closed. Some can be system modals, meaning that no further operations can be performed on the machine until the dialog is closed. Quite often, these dialogs offer various options presented as buttons, such as **OK**, **Approve**, **Submit**, **Apply**, **Cancel**, **Ignore**, and **Retry**. This variety needs to be managed in a very accurate fashion, as the choice made affects the rest of the test flow substantially. Moreover, sometimes another pop-up dialog may show up as a direct result of a given choice. Such an event may be delayed a bit, for example, due to server-side validation, and hence it is of utmost importance to detect it in a reliable yet efficient way.

The basic problem with pop-up dialogs is that, quite often, their appearance is unexpected. For instance, if there is some script error as a result of a bug, then a dialog will appear, but our script would not know how to handle it unless we put that logic or intelligence into the code. If we fail to do so, then our script will make a futile attempt to continue the normal flow, and hence, precious time and resources would be lost. On the other hand, in such a case, we would like our script to detect such an error dialog and report that a problem may have been found. Perhaps we would like to exit that specific action or test, or even halt the whole run session.

One way of handling unexpected pop-up dialogs is using the UFT built-in recovery scenario feature. However, in my view, this practice is not recommended due to performance issues and implementation complexity. Hence, it will not be covered here. Instead, we will suggest a generic technique that is very simple to implement and can be custom tailored to any specific requirement that may arise.

Getting ready

From the **File** menu, navigate to **New** | **Function Library** or use the *Alt + Shift + N* shortcut. Name the new function library `Web_Functions.vbs`.

How to do it...

If we refrain from using the recovery scenario feature as I recommended, then the question remains, how can we have any pop-up dialog appearance covered with the least amount of code? If we take the risk of such dialogs too seriously, then we may end up with our code cluttered with `If-Then-End If` statements, just to check that our application context is normal and no pop-up dialog is opened.

The approach I will advocate here assumes that the risk of unexpected pop-up dialogs (for instance, due to bugs) for a mature application is minimal. So instead of listening to pop-up dialogs all the time (as is the case for a recovery scenario), we will check if there is a pop-up dialog open, just in case an operation fails. For example, if we try to click on an object on a web page while a pop-up dialog is open, a runtime error will be thrown by UFT. To prevent a UFT pop-up dialog from opening and hence pausing the run session, we will catch the error inside our code. After the pop-up dialog is handled (closed), our test will continue, stop, or reroute the flow according to the analysis of the situation. Here, we shall assume that the dialog is not consequential to the flow, and that just closing it solves the problem.

To implement our solution, we need to do two basic things:

- ▶ Write one generic function, `DialogHandler()`, which can detect and handle any open dialog.

▸ Catch an error in certain methods (where the presence of a pop-up dialog would affect the flow) and invoke the `dialogHandler()` method. Here we will be using the `RegisterUserFunc` technique explained in detail in *Chapter 4, Method Overriding*.

We will then write the following method to handle any pop-up dialog in our `library Web_Functions.vbs` function:

```
Function handleDialog()
    Dim sMessageText

    'A popup dialog can be directly accessed but in some cases its
      parent Browser may be required
    'For instance: Browser("micclass:=Browser").Dialog("regexpwndcla
ss:=#32770")
    With Dialog("regexpwndclass:=#32770")
        'Check if a Dialog exists
        If .Exist(0) Then
            'Focus on the Dialog
            .Activate
            'Get the static text
            sMessageText= .Static("regexpwndtitle:=.+").
GetTOProperty("text")
            'Click on the OK button (can be parameterized in case
              of need)
            .WinButton("text:=OK").Click
            'Check again to verify that the Dialog was closed
            If not .Exist(0) Then
                Reporter.ReportEvent micPass, "handleDialog",
                    "Dialog with message '" & sMessageText & "
                    ' was closed."
                handleDialog=true
            else
                Reporter.ReportEvent micFail, "handleDialog",
                    "Dialog with message '" & sMessageText & "
                    ' was not closed."
                handleDialog=false
            End If
        else
            'No dialog was found so we return true
            handleDialog=true
        End If
    End With
End Function
```

As an example, we will write the following overriding method in our `Web_RegisteredFunctions.vbs` function library:

```
Function WebEdit_Set(obj, text)
    On error resume next
    'Try
    obj.set text
    'Catch
    if err.number <> 0 then
        'If there's a dialog open that is handled then retry.
        if handleDialog() then
            obj.set text
        else
            Reporter.ReportEvent micFail, "WebEdit_Set", "An error
                occurred while attempting to set " & text & " to the
                input. No dialog found or dialog could not be
                handled properly."
            'Stop the run session (or handle otherwise)
            ExitTest()
        End if
    End if
End Function
```

Of course, here we assume that closing the dialog is a good enough solution, but this may not be the case. If a script error caused the browser to open a pop-up dialog, then it may reopen. In such a case, a more sophisticated scheme would be required, which is out of the scope of this basic recipe. Another thing that is worth noting is that if the `HandleDialog()` method does not find any dialog open, it is up to the calling function or action to check for other possible problems that caused the error. As mentioned earlier, the modal dialog may be implemented as a `Div` element, so the inline descriptive programming-based description would not fit.

> The previous function serves only as an example of how to implement the approach outlined in this recipe. Of course, the same logic should be implemented for each operation (click, double-click, and so on) that can be blocked by a pop-up dialog.

We will register the previous `WebEdit_Set` method before starting the test flow and unregister it at the end of the flow (refer to *Chapter 4, Method Overriding*):

```
RegisterUserFunc "WebEdit", "Set", "WebEdit_Set"

'Test Flow goes here...

UnregisterUserFunc "WebEdit", "Set"
```

How it works...

The `HandleDialog()` function uses a generic description to identify a dialog and close an open one. Of course, this is a simplified version and may need to be expanded. For instance, to make the function able to also handle application modal pop-up dialogs built on web `Div` elements with JavaScript, one should add suitable working code with a matching description. In addition, the function is built on the assumption that there is an **OK** button to close the dialog. This, however, may not be the case, and dialogs with more than a single button would require a more elaborate method.

The overriding `WebEdit_Set(obj, text)` method is an example of how to achieve the effect of detecting an obstructing open modal dialog. First, we disable the automatic runtime mechanism for error handling with `On Error Resume Next`. Next, we try to perform the operation on the input field. If the operation fails, the error is trapped and `HandleDialog()` is invoked.

Downloading a file using XMLHttp

This recipe will show you how to download a file using the `XMLHttp` object, which we have seen in action in the *Checking whether page links are broken* recipe. Here we will expand on a theme and see how to synchronize our script using the `onreadystatechange` event handler to report on the progress of our download. The code includes the required modifications, and is the same as the one I used in a project a few years ago.

Getting ready

From the **File** menu, navigate to **New | Function Library** or use the *Alt + Shift + N* shortcut. Name the new function library as `Web_Download.vbs`. To use the `AutoItX` COM object, go to `https://www.autoitscript.com/site/autoit/downloads/` to download and install AutoIt. This is absolutely necessary in order to ensure that the code given here will work properly with regard to the notifications display.

How to do it...

This recipe will demonstrate how to download the last build JAR file from a remote build machine and deploy it to the local machine. This is very useful to automate daily build updates and trigger automated tests to check the new build for sanity. Please take note that this solution comprises several components and is quite complex to grasp:

- The `Http` class, which handles the download operation
- The `StateChangeHandler` class, which listens to the `onreadystatechange` event and handles notifications about the progress

- The `AutoIt` class, which is a utility wrapper for the `AutoItX` COM object

- The `App_GetLastBuild` class, which controls the whole process

Proceed with the following steps:

1. First, we will define the following constants in the function library (of course, it would be better that at least some of these values be stored as `Environment` variables):

```
const S_OK = 0
const APP_PATH = "C:\Program Files\MyApp"
const DOWNLOAD_PATH = "C:\Documents and Settings\admin\My
   Documents\Downloads\"
const BUILD_PATH = "http://repository.app:8081/builds/last/"
const TMP_JAR = "App-1.0.0-build1.jar"
const APP_JAR = "App.jar"
const RES_ZIP = "App-1.0.0-build1-resources.zip"
```

 The preceding values are for illustration purposes only.

2. The next step is to write the `Http` class to handle the download process. The process is explained as follows:

   ❑ First we will define the fields:

   ```
   class Http
       Public m_objXMLHttp'The XMLHttp object
       Private m_objHandler 'Stores a reference to the handler
         of the event onreadystatechange
       Private m_strLocalfilename 'Name of local filename
       Private m_strUrl 'Address of download location
   ```

   ❑ Next, we will write the initialization and termination subroutines for the class:

   ```
   private sub class_initialize
           Handler = new StateChangeHandler
           Handler.Http = Me
           XML = createobject("MSXML2.XMLHTTP")
       end sub

       private sub class_terminate
           Handler = Nothing
           XML = Nothing
       end sub
   ```

❑ Then, we will write the properties for the class that will provide access to the fields. Note especially the XMLHttp property, which is used to assign the XMLHttp object to the m_objXMLHttp field and also to set the StateChangeHandler object to the object's onreadystatechange event.

```
public property get XML
        set XML = m_objXML
    end property
    private property let XML(byref objXML)
        set m_objXML = objXML

        if typename(objXML) <> "Nothing" then _
                m_objXML.onreadystatechange = Handler
    end property
```

❑ Other properties of the class are quite trivial, just being accessors to the fields:

```
public property get LocalFilename
        LocalFilename = m_strLocalfilename
    end property
    private property let LocalFilename(byval strFilename)
        m_strLocalfilename = strFilename
    end property

    public property get Filename
        Filename =
          createobject("Scripting.FileSystemObject")
          .GetFileName(Localfilename)
    end property

    public property get URL
        URL = m_strUrl
    end property
    private property let URL(byval strUrl)
        m_strUrl = strUrl
    end property

    private property get Handler
        set Handler = m_objHandler
    end property
    private property let Handler(byref objHandler)
        set m_objHandler = objHandler
    end property
```

❑ The `DownBinFile` method handles the process as shown in the following code:

```
public function DownBinFile(byval strURL, byval
  strDownloadPath)
        const adTypeBinary = 1
        const adModeReadWrite = 3
          const adSaveCreateOverwrite = 2

          dim arrTmp, oStream, intStatus, FSO, strInfo

        arrTmp = Split(strURL, "/")
        URL = strURL
        LocalFilename = strDownloadPath & Unescape(arrTmp(UB
ound(arrTmp)))

          if XML.open("GET", strURL, false) = S_OK then
            XML.send

            set oStream = createobject("ADODB.Stream")
            with oStream
                .type = adTypeBinary
                .mode = adModeReadWrite
                .open
                do Until XML.readyState = 4
                    Wscript.Sleep 500
                Loop
                .write XML.responseBody
                .SaveToFile LocalFilename,
adSaveCreateOverwrite

                strInfo = "Download of file '" & strURL &
                  "' finished with "
                set FSO = createobject("Scripting.
FileSystemObject")
                if FSO.FileExists(LocalFilename) then
                    strInfo = strInfo & "success."
                    DownBinFile = 0
                else
                    strInfo = strInfo & "failure."
                    DownBinFile = 1
                end if
                with oAutoIt.Object
```

```
                          .ToolTip strInfo, 1100, 1000
                          .Sleep 7000
                          .ToolTip("")
                    end with
                end with 'ADODB.Stream
                set oStream = Nothing
            else
                XML.abort
                strInfo = "Send download command to server
                    failed" & vbNewLine & XML.statusText
                with oAutoIt.Object
                    call .ToolTip(strInfo, 1100, 1000)
                    .Sleep 7000
                    call .ToolTip("")
                end with
                exit function
            end if
        end function
    end class
```

3. The `Http` class here refers to `StateChangeHandler`, which in turn uses the `AutoItX` COM object to display a notification to inform about the progress of the download process.

    The `Exec` method is defined as `Public Default` so that it is automatically triggered when the object is referenced. As an instance of this object is assigned to the `onreadystatechange` event of the `Http` request object, every time `readystate` changes, this function is performed to display the updated data on the download process in the notification area on the taskbar.

```
class StateChangeHandler
    public m_objHttp

    public default function Exec()
        dim strInfo, intDelay

        intDelay = 0
        strInfo = "State changed: " & Http.XML.readyState &
            vbNewLine & "Downloading file: " & Http.Filename
        Select Case Http.XML.readyState
            Case "3"
                strInfo = strInfo & vbNewLine & "Please
                    wait..."
            Case "4"
```

```
                    strInfo = strInfo & vbNewLine & "Finished.
                       Total " & len(Http.XML.responseBody)\512
                          & "KB downloaded."
                    intDelay = 1500
              Case else
          End Select
          'with AutoIt
          with oAutoIt.Object
              .ToolTip strInfo, 1100, 1000
               .Sleep 500+intDelay
               .ToolTip("")
           end with
       end function


       public property get Http
           set Http = m_objHttp
       end property
       public property let Http(byval objHttp)
           set m_objHttp = objHttp
       end property
   end class
```

4. The `AutoItX` COM object is wrapped by the `AutoIt` class for easier use:

```
class AutoIt
    private m_oAutoIt

    public default property Get Object
        set Object = m_oAutoIt
    end property
    private property let Object(byval AutoItX)
        set m_oAutoIt = AutoItX
    end property

    private sub class_initialize
        Object = createobject("AutoItX3.Control")
    end sub
    private sub class_terminate
        Object = Nothing
    end sub
end class
```

5. Finally, the next `App_GetLastBuild` class controls the whole process. The whole process is explained as follows:

- First, we define the fields as follows:

```
class App_GetLastBuild
        private oHttp
        private Status
        private FSO
        private FoldersToDelete 'Local folders to delete'
        private ResourcesZIP
        private OrigJar
        private DestJar
        private BuildPath
        private ExtractPath
```

- Then, we define a method that will assign these fields the value:

```
public function SetArgs()
        FoldersToDelete = Array(APP_PATH & "\images",
          APP_PATH & "\properties", APP_PATH & "\wizards")
        ResourcesZIP = RES_ZIP
        OrigJar = TMP_JAR
        DestJar = APP_JAR
        ExtractPath = APP_PATH
        BuildPath = BUILD_PATH
    end function
```

- Next, we define the `Exec` method as default; a method that will control the whole process:

```
public default function Exec()
        call SetArgs()

        '1) Delete local folders
        DeleteFolders(FoldersToDelete)

        '2) Download resources zip
        Status = oHttp.DownBinFile(BUILD_PATH &
          ResourcesZIP, DOWNLOAD_PATH)
        if Status <> 0 then exit function
        'Extract the resources
        call ExtractZipFile(DOWNLOAD_PATH & ResourcesZIP,
          APP_PATH)
        'Delete resources zip
        FSO.DeleteFile(DOWNLOAD_PATH & ResourcesZIP)
```

```
'3) Delete main GUI jar
FSO.DeleteFile(APP_PATH & "\lib\" & DestJar)

'4) Download the updated GUI jar
Status = oHttp.DownBinFile(BUILD_PATH & OrigJar,
  DOWNLOAD_PATH)
if Status <> 0 then exit function
'Copy the updated GUI jar
call FSO.CopyFile(DOWNLOAD_PATH & OrigJar, APP_PATH
  & "\lib\", true)
'Rename GUI jar
call FSO.MoveFile(APP_PATH & "\lib\" & OrigJar,
  APP_PATH & "\lib\" & DestJar)

'Delete the downloaded GUI jar
FSO.DeleteFile(DOWNLOAD_PATH & OrigJar)
end function
```

❑ We then define the method to delete folders (for cleanup purposes before downloading):

```
public function DeleteFolders(byval arrFolders)
    dim ix

    for ix = 0 To UBound(arrFolders)
        if FSO.FolderExists(arrFolders(ix)) then
            FSO.DeleteFile(arrFolders(ix) & "\*.*")
            FSO.DeleteFolder(arrFolders(ix))
        end if
    next
end function
```

❑ Next, we define a method to uncompress a ZIP file:

```
public function ExtractZipFile(byval strZIPFile, byval
  strExtractToPath)
    dim objShellApp
    dim WsShell
    dim objZippedFiles

    set objShellApp = createobject("Shell.Application")
    set WsShell = createobject("Wscript.Shell")
```

```
          set objZippedFiles = objShellApp.
NameSpace(strZIPFile).items

          objShellApp.NameSpace(strExtractToPath).
CopyHere(objZippedF
   iles)

          'Free Objects
          set objZippedFiles = Nothing
          set objShellApp = Nothing
     end function
```

❑   Then we define the initialization and termination subroutines:

```
private sub class_initialize
          set FSO = createobject("Scripting.FileSystemObject")
          set oHttp = new Http
     end sub
     private sub class_terminate
          set FSO = Nothing
          set oHttp = Nothing
     end sub
end class
```

6.   In `Action1`, the following code will launch the download process:

```
dim oAutoIt
dim oDownload

set oAutoIt = new AutoIt
set oDownload = new App_GetLastBuild

oDownload.Exec

set oDownload = Nothing
Set oAutoIt = nothing
```

How it works...

As mentioned in the previous section, the solution involves a complex architecture using VBScript classes and several COM objects (`AutoItX`, `FileSystemObject`, `ADODB.Stream`, and so on). A detailed explanation of this architecture is provided here.

Let us start with the main process in `Action1` and then delve into the intricacies of our more complex architecture. The first step involves the instantiation of two of our custom classes, namely, `AutoIt` and `App_GetLastBuild`. After our objects are already loaded and initialized, we call `objDownload.Exec`, which triggers and controls the whole download scenario. In this method we do the following:

- ▸ Initialize the class fields.
- ▸ Delete the local folders.
- ▸ Download the binary resources file. We check if the returned status is OK; if it is otherwise, we exit the function.
- ▸ After the download process ends, we extract the contents of the ZIP file to the application path, and then delete the ZIP file.

We then start the process for the main JAR file as follows:

- ▸ Delete the old file.
- ▸ Download the JAR file. We check if the returned status is OK; if it is otherwise, we exit the function.
- ▸ After the download process ends, we copy the file to the target location and rename it (assuming the last build main JAR file always carries the same name, regardless of the version).

Now, let us examine what happens behind the scenes after the two classes are instantiated, as mentioned in this section.

The `AutoIt` class automatically instantiates the `AutoItX.Control` object through its `Private Sub Class_Initialize` subroutine. The `App_GetLastBuild` class, through its own `Sub Class_Initialize`, automatically creates these objects, namely, a `Scripting.FileSystemObject` object and an instance of our `Http` custom class.

Let us take a close look at the `Sub Class_Initialize` of the `Http` class:

```
private sub class_initialize
    Handler = new StateChangeHandler
    Handler.Http = Me
    XML = createobject("MSXML2.XMLHTTP")
end sub
```

Here we can see a strange thing. Our `Http` object creates an instance of the `StateChangeHandler` class and immediately assigns the `Http` property of the `Handler` object a reference to itself) `Handler.Http = me`). That is, the parent object (`Http`) has a reference to the child object (`StateChangeHandler`) and the latter has a reference to the parent object stored in its `Http` property. The purpose of this seemingly strange design is to enable interoperability between both objects.

Finally, an instance of XMLHttp is created. As seen in our recipe, on checking for broken links, this object provides the services we need to manage communication with a web server through the HTTP protocol. Here, however, there is something extra because we want to notify the end user about the progress of the download. Let us take a closer look at the way this instantiation is handled:

```
private property let XML(byref objXML)
        set m_objXML = objXML

        if typename(objXML) <> "Nothing" then _
                m_objXML.onreadystatechange = Handler
    end property
```

We pass the XMLHttp object created in our Sub Class_Initialize subroutine and check if it is a real object (which it always should be because of the way we have designed our code). Then, we implicitly assign our handler's default method to the XMLHttp event onreadystatechange. Recall that a public default function in a VBScript class is executed whenever an object instance of the class is referenced without explicitly calling a method or property using the dot operator. This way, whenever the readystate property of the XMLHttp object changes, the default Exec method of the StateChangeHandler object is automatically executed, and a notification about the status of the process is displayed using the AutoIt COM object. Just one thing is missing from our code, a check of the Http status after XMLHttp.send and later on.

Checking whether a website is up

This recipe will show you how to check that a site is up, using the XMLHttp object we have seen in action in the *Checking whether page links are broken* recipe.

Getting ready

We will be using the Web_Functions.vbs function library, seen in the previous recipe, to take advantage of the objXMLHttp global variable, along with the InitXMLHttp() and DisposeXMLHttp() functions. Make sure the library is associated to the test.

How to do it...

Basically, here we will follow the same logic as in the *Checking whether page links are broken* recipe, but instead of getting the URL from the page links dynamically, we will just pass the URL to the function:

```
Function checkSiteIsUp(URL)
    If lcase(typename(oXMLHttp)) <> "xmlhttp" Then
```

```
            initXMLHttp()
        End If

        if oXMLHttp.open("GET", URL, false) = 0 then
            oXMLHttp.send()

            If oXMLHttp.Status<>200 Then
                reporter.ReportEvent micFail, "Check site is up",
                    "Site " & URL & " is unreachable: " &
                    oXMLHttp.Status
            Else
                reporter.ReportEvent micPass, " Check site is up ",
                    "Site " & URL & " is up"
            End If
        End if
    End Function
```

In `Action1`, we will invoke the function as follows:

```
checkSiteIsUp("http://www.advancedqtp.com")
```

How it works...

As mentioned in this recipe, the logic here is pretty much the same as with checking for broken links. We send an `Http Get` request and check the status returned by the server.

See also

The *Checking whether page links are broken* recipe.

Uploading a file using FTP

In a previous recipe, we have seen how to download a file using `XMLHttp`. Here we will see how to upload a file to a web server using the FTP protocol.

Getting ready

From the **File** menu, navigate to **New | Function Library** or use the *Alt + Shift + N* shortcut. Name the new function library `FTP.vbs`. Make sure the library is associated to the test. In order to use the code given in this recipe, you must have an FTP user account on a server. To understand this recipe, you should be familiar with FTP protocol and the command line.

How to do it...

In the function library, we will put the following code.

1. First we will define the following constants for better readability and reusability:

```
const C_FSO="Scripting.FileSystemObject"
const C_SHELL="WScript.Shell"
const C_ASCII="ascii", C_BIN="binary"
const C_FTP_CMD="%comspec% /c FTP -n -s:"
const C_SYNC_TIME=5000
const C_TEMP="%TEMP%"
const C_OPENASDEFAULT=-2
const C_FAIL_IFNOT_EXIST=0
const C_FORREADING=1
const C_FORWRITING=2
const C_QUIT="quit"
const C_PROMPT="prompt n"
const C_PUT_OP="put "
const C_CD_OP="cd "
const C_FILE_TRANSFER_OK="226-File successfully transferred"
const C_FILE_NOT_FOUND="File not found"
const C_CANNOT_LOGIN="Cannot log in"
const C_UNKNOWN_ERROR="Unknown error"
const C_USER="USER "
const C_REDIRECT=" > "
const C_ERR_STR="Error: "
```

2. Next, we will define our `FTP` class with the following fields, which will be used to store the data needed for the FTP operation:

```
class FTP
    private m_oFSO
    private m_oScriptShell

    private m_sLocalFile
    private m_sPassword
    private m_sRemotePath
    private m_sResultsTmpFilename
    private m_sScriptTmpFilename
    private m_sSite
    private m_sTType
    private m_sUsername
```

3. We will then initialize our class upon instantiation with a `FileSystemObject` to handle files and a `WScript.Shell` object to handle commands:

```
private sub class_initialize
        FSO=CreateObject(C_FSO)
            ScriptShell=CreateObject(C_SHELL)
            'default transfer type - binary
            TType=C_BIN
        end sub
```

4. We will take care of disposing of the same objects at the time the object is destroyed:

```
private sub class_terminate
        FSO=nothing
            ScriptShell=nothing
        end sub
```

5. Then we will initialize the object with our FTP account connection and login information:

```
function init(sSite, sUsername, sPassword)
            Site=sSite
        Username=C_USER & sUsername
        Password=sPassword
        end function
```

6. Next, upload the local file with the following method:

```
function uploadFile(sLocalFile, sRemotePath, sTType)
        LocalFile=C_PUT_OP & sLocalFile
          RemotePath=C_CD_OP & sRemotePath
          TType=sTType


        me.createFTPScript()
'Run the FTP command through the command line
'we use the WScript.Shell object to run the FTP command
'through the command line, in which the -n switch
'suppresses auto-login upon initial connection and the -s:
'switch takes the path of the temporary script file we
'created as parameter. The commands contained in such a
'file run automatically after FTP starts. The > operator
'redirects the FTP verbose output to our temporary results
'file. The last parameter is set to TRUE and it indicates
'whether to wait until the FTP program finishes.
ScriptShell.Run C_FTP_CMD & ScriptTmpFilename & " " & Site
  & C_REDIRECT & ResultsTmpFilename, 0, TRUE
```

```
        Wait 0, C_SYNC_TIME

        uploadFile=me.checkResults()

        if FSO.FileExists(ScriptTmpFilename) then
            FSO.DeleteFile(ScriptTmpFilename)
        end if
    end function
```

7. Check the results of the transfer, which are stored in `ResultsTmpFile` with the following method:

```
function checkResults()
        dim fFTPResults, sResults

        'Check results of transfer.
        Set fFTPResults = FSO.OpenTextFile(ResultsTmpFilename, C_
FORREADING,
    C_FAIL_IFNOT_EXIST, C_OPENASDEFAULT)
        if not fFTPResults.AtEndOfStream then
            sResults = fFTPResults.ReadAll
        end if
        fFTPResults.Close

        if FSO.FileExists(ResultsTmpFilename) then
            FSO.DeleteFile(ResultsTmpFilename)
        end if

        If InStr(sResults, C_FILE_TRANSFER_OK) > 0 Then
          checkResults = micPass
        ElseIf InStr(sResults, C_FILE_NOT_FOUND) > 0 Then
          checkResults = micFail
          sResults=C_ERR_STR&C_FILE_NOT_FOUND&vbNewLine&sResults
        ElseIf InStr(sResults, C_CANNOT_LOGIN) > 0 Then
          checkResults = micFail
          sResults=C_ERR_STR&C_CANNOT_LOGIN&vbNewLine&sResults
        Else
          checkResults = micFail '"Error: Unknown."
          sResults=C_ERR_STR&C_UNKNOWN_ERROR&vbNewLine&sResults
        End If

        reporter.ReportEvent checkResults, typename(me) &
          ".uploadFile", sResults
    end function
```

8. The `CreateFTPScript()` function creates the FTP script from the input file `fFTPScript`:

```
function createFTPScript()
        dim fFTPScript          'As file
        dim sFTPScript          'As string
        dim sFTPTempPath     'As string
        dim sFTPTempFile     'As string

        'Input file for ftp command
        sFTPScript=join(array(Username, Password,
          RemotePath, TType, C_PROMPT, LocalFile, C_QUIT,
          C_QUIT, C_QUIT), vbNewLine)

        sFTPTempPath = ScriptShell.ExpandEnvironmentStrings(C_
TEMP)

        ScriptTmpFilename = sFTPTempPath & "\" &
          FSO.GetTempName
        ResultsTmpFilename = sFTPTempPath & "\" &
          FSO.GetTempName

        'Write the input file for the ftp command to a
          temporary file.
        Set fFTPScript = FSO.CreateTextFile(ScriptTmpFilename,
True)
        fFTPScript.WriteLine(sFTPScript)
        fFTPScript.Close
        Set fFTPScript = Nothing
    end function
```

9. Add the following properties as accessors to the fields:

```
public property get FSO()
        set FSO=m_oFSO
    end property
    public property let FSO(oFSO)
        set m_oFSO=oFSO
    end property

    public property get LocalFile()
        LocalFile=m_sLocalFile
    end property
    public property let LocalFile(sLocalFile)
        m_sLocalFile=sLocalFile
    end property
```

```
public property get Password()
    Password=m_sPassword
end property
public property let Password(sPassword)
    m_sPassword=sPassword
end property

public property get RemotePath()
    RemotePath=m_sRemotePath
end property
public property let RemotePath(sRemotePath)
    m_sRemotePath=sRemotePath
end property

public property get ResultsTmpFilename()
    ResultsTmpFilename=m_sResultsTmpFilename
end property
public property let ResultsTmpFilename(sResultsTmpFilename)
    m_sResultsTmpFilename=sResultsTmpFilename
end property

public property get ScriptTmpFilename()
    ScriptTmpFilename=m_sScriptTmpFilename
end property
public property let ScriptTmpFilename(sScriptTmpFilename)
    m_sScriptTmpFilename=sScriptTmpFilename
end property

public property get ScriptShell()
    set ScriptShell=m_oScriptShell
end property
public property let ScriptShell(oScriptShell)
    set m_oScriptShell=oScriptShell
end property

public property get Site()
    Site=m_sSite
end property
public property let Site(sSite)
    m_sSite=sSite
end property

public property get TType()
    TType=m_sTType
end property
public property let TType(sTType)
```

```
            select case lcase(sTType)
                case C_ASCII, C_BIN
                    m_sTType=lcase(sTType)
                case else
                     m_sTType=C_BIN
            end select
        end property

        public property get Username()
            Username=m_sUsername
        end property
        public property let Username(sUsername)
            m_sUsername=sUsername
        end property
end class
```

The GetFTP method is used as a constructor for the FTP object:

```
function getFTP(sSite, sUsername, sPassword)
    dim oFTP
    on error resume next
    set oFTP=new FTP
     call oFTP.init(sSite, sUsername, sPassword)
     if err.number<>0 then set oFTP=nothing
     set getFTP=oFTP
end function
```

10. Finally, in `Action1`, we will invoke the FTP upload function with the following code, which creates an FTP custom object (based on our class) and uploads the file.

```
dim sSite, sUsername, sPassword, sLocalFile, sRemotePath

sSite="www.mysite.com"
sUsername="admin"
sPassword="mypassword"
sLocalFile="mylocalpathname\" & "mylocalfile.txt"
sRemotePath="//ftp/admin/"

set oFTP=getFTP(sSite, sUsername, sPassword)
if not oFTP is nothing then
    call oFTP.uploadFile(sLocalFile, sRemotePath, "")
    set OFTP=nothing
else
    reporter.ReportEvent micFail, "FTP.uploadFile", "Could
      not create FTP object."
end if
```

How it works...

First, we define the five variables required by the FTP protocol:

- ▶ `strSite`: This is the URL of our FTP server
- ▶ `strUsername`: This is the name of our FTP account
- ▶ `strPassword`: This is the password for our FTP account
- ▶ `strLocalFile`: This is the file to be uploaded
- ▶ `strRemotePath`: This is the path on our FTP account in which we put our file

We then retrieve an instance of our `FTP` class by calling the `getFTP` method with three arguments, namely, `strSite`, `strUsername`, and `strPassword`. A check is performed to verify that a valid object was returned, and then the `uploadFile` method is called with two arguments, `strLocalFile` and `strRemotePath`.

In the `uploadFile` method, we use these arguments to build a string with the FTP commands required to perform the upload operation. The transfer type is validated (ASCII or binary) in the `TType` property, with binary as the default type. A call to `createFTPScript` writes this string to a temporary file, which then serves as input script for the FTP command. We also create a temporary filename to store the results of the upload operation.

Next, we use the `WScript.Shell` object to run the FTP command through the command line, in which the `-n` switch suppresses auto login upon initial connection, and the `-s` switch takes the path of the temporary script file that we created as parameter. The commands contained in such a file run automatically after FTP starts. The `>` operator redirects the FTP verbose output to our temporary results file. The last parameter is set to `TRUE`, and it indicates whether to wait until the FTP program finishes or not. After it does, we call `checkResults()` to read the contents of the output file and return whether our upload was successful or not according to the status returned by FTP, which is written to the file.

Identifying elements based on anchors

In some cases, the same web element is used more than once in a page. For example, suppose that the application uses a toggle button implemented using an image to change the value or the state of other elements, such as input controls (for example, `WebEdit`). Further, let us assume that these elements possess exactly the same set of attributes, and that they have no unique ID or name to reckon upon for unequivocal identification. In such a case, the task of identifying these objects during runtime can be achieved using alternative options given by UFT, such as the index or location of the object. However, this solution is not robust enough, as I discovered in one of the projects in which I was involved.

The problem was found precisely with such toggle buttons. At first, work was done relying on the index (because the page layout was fixed), but soon I discovered that in some cases, QTP clicked on the wrong button (the project was done in 2007-2008 with QTP 9.5). After investigating the issue, it turned out that there was a bug in the application. Though the intended toggle operation was indeed executed, in some cases, the image of the toggled button did not change. As a result, all elements with an index greater than the unchanged element remained with an index greater than expected. To illustrate the problem, suppose that we have 10 such controls in a page, and we click on the third control (index = 2). Now, as we expected the original image collection to decrease by one, reference to index = 2 should have led to click on the **Next Image** button. However, as the image was not replaced to reflect the new state of the element, the index = 2 continued to reference the same element! So, the script got stuck on that control, clicking again and again. There was also a checkpoint that verified that clicking on the toggle button actually switched the values of two input elements, and of course, these never changed, as the wrong toggle button was clicked!

After facing such a bug (which was reported, of course) a dilemma arose. Should we stop the run session or find a workaround to continue after reporting the problem? The decision was quite easy, because the bug was considered minor. So we opted for the second alternative.

How to do it...

In automation, we usually refrain from identifying TOs based on their location on the screen. Absolute coordinates are really bad identifiers, as the screen resolution can change (and also modern browsers have zooming capabilities). In addition, using *abs_x* and *abs_y* would be sensitive to any tiny layout change. However, if we know how to identify an object based on its name, ID, or inner text, to name a few valid properties, then we can use it as an anchor to identify other related objects in its vicinity. The idea is similar to that of attached text, which was accustomed in older technologies. Actually, a label was identified, and then, the target input control was identified based on a search algorithm for text to its left or top.

The idea was quite simple. First, get the collection of objects to search (in our case, it was a collection of images). Second, get a reference to the target anchor object (input element `WebEdit` by QTP/UFT). Finally, in the collection, find the one object that is closest to the anchor (in our case, they were always aligned vertically, that is, at about the same height, so the proximity was calculated along the *x* axis).

From these lines of reasoning, the following code emerged:

```
Const C_SEARCH_RANGE = 35 'Pixels

Function getObjectByAnchor(oParent, oTargetDesc, oAnchor)
    Dim i, oCollection
    Dim AnchorX, AnchorY, TargetX, TargetY
```

```
'Set the function to return nothing in case of failure
Set getObjectByAnchor=nothing

'Get the collection of candidate target objects
Set oCollection = oParent.ChildObjects(oTargetDesc)

'Check if the given description yielded an empty collection
If oCollection.count = 0 Then
    Reporter.ReportEvent micWarning, "getObjectByAnchor", "No
      object matched the given description"
    Exit function
End If

'Get the Anchor's position
With oAnchor
    AnchorX=.GetROProperty("abs_x")
    AnchorY=.GetROProperty("abs_y")
End With

'Search the collection of candidate objects
For i = 0 To oCollection.count-1
    Set oTarget=oCollection(i)
    'Get the object's position
    With oTarget
        TargetX=.GetROProperty("abs_x")
        TargetY=.GetROProperty("abs_y")
    End With
    'Check if the objects are vertically aligned (along the Y
      axis)
    If TargetY=AnchorY Then
        'Check if it the objects are close enough (within a
          range defined in the global constant C_SEARCH_RANGE)
        If abs(TargetX-AnchorX) <= C_SEARCH_RANGE Then
            'Return the current candidate object as target
            set getObjectByAnchor=oTarget
            Exit Function
        End If
    End If
Next
End Function
```

In `Action1`, we would call the `GetObjectByAnchor` function as follows:

```
dim ele, oParent, oTargetDesc, oAnchor

Set oParent=Browser("title:=.*Advanced QTP.*").Page("title:=.+")
Set oTargetDesc=Description.Create()
oTargetDesc("micclass").Value="Image"
oAnchor=oParent.WebEdit("name:=s")
set ele = getObjectByAnchor(oParent, oTargetDesc, oAnchor)
If not ele is nothing Then
    ele.click
else
    reporter.ReportEvent micFail, "Click on Image", "No matching
object was found."
    exittest
End If
```

> Recall that in VBScript, the value `Nothing` is an object, so it is not enough to check the returned value with `If Not IsObject(ele) Then`. Therefore, we used a less common syntax, namely, `If Not ele Is Nothing Then`.

How it works...

The `GetObjectByAnchor` function accepts the following three arguments:

- `objParent`: This is a reference to the parent object or container of the elements from which we need to find our target element
- `objTargetDesc`: This is a description object carrying the properties and values pairs used to retrieve the collection of candidate target elements
- `objAnchor`: This is a reference to the element to which the target element is expected to be aligned

This function requires the execution of the following steps:

- Get the collection of candidate target objects. If empty, report and exit the function while returning the VBScript value of `Nothing`.
- Get the position of `objAnchor`.

▶ Loop through the collection of candidate objects and do as follows for each of them:

❏ Get the position of `oTarget` (which is assigned the current `oCollection` item `i`).

❏ Check if `oTarget` is vertically aligned (along the *y* axis) with respect to `objAnchor`.

❏ If it is vertically aligned, then check if, with respect to `objAnchor`, `oTarget` is within the search range we defined in the `C_SEARCH_RANGE` global constant.

❏ If it's within the range, then `oTarget` is most probably the object we are looking for. So exit the function while returning `oTarget`; if not, continue searching.

In `Action1`, we get the value returned by the function and proceed accordingly. If the value is not `Nothing`, then we click on the element. Otherwise, we report on a failure to find a matching object and stop the test.

Synchronizing a test with a web page loading

An essential requirement from any automated test script is that it must synchronize with **Application Under Test** (**AUT**). This is especially true for GUI automation, because the test script actually attempts to emulate the actions that a human user would perform on the application's front end. Hence, it is of utmost importance to take care that operations on a page are carried out when the controls are fully loaded and ready to accept inputs.

How to do it...

All web classes, `Page`, `WebEdit`, `WebButton`, `Image`, and so on, provide an attribute that indicates the state of the element. This attribute is `readystate`, and its value ranges from 0 (uninitialized) to 4 (complete). So basically, to synchronize our script with the full loading of a web element, we need to wait until its `readystate` attribute reaches the value of 4.

The following generic function accepts an element and a timeout period, and it waits until the element reaches the load complete state or timeout:

```
Function WaitUntilComplete(o, timeout)
    Dim iElapsed
```

```
            WaitUntilComplete=true
            iElapsed=0
            Do while o.Object.readystate <> 4
                wait 0, C_INTERVAL_MSEC
                iElapsed=iElapsed+C_INTERVAL_MSEC
                If iElapsed > timeout Then
                    reporter.ReportEvent micWarning, "WaitUntilComplete",
    "Element did not load within " & timeout & " msec."
                    WaitUntilComplete=false
                    Exit Do
                End If
            Loop
    End Function
```

We will call the function in `Action1` as follows:

```
    Dim bPageComplete

    bPageComplete=WaitUntilComplete(Browser("title:=.*Advanced
      QTP.*").Page("title:=.+"), 2000)
```

How it works...

The `WaitUntilComplete` function takes two arguments, the object to synchronize with and the maximum time we are prepared to wait in milliseconds. We initialize this function optimistically, and then loop while the native `readystate` attribute is not equal to 4 (complete), waiting for an interval of `200` milliseconds each time, as defined in the `C_INTERVAL_MSEC` constant. The `iElapsed` variable increases with each cycle, and a check is performed to see if it reaches the timeout. If it reaches timeout, we exit the `Do` loop after assigning the function to return the value `False`. If `true` is returned, then it means that the complete state was reached before the timeout; therefore, our test can continue as planned.

The `readystate` attribute is accessed through the element's `Object` property, which provides access to the native properties and methods of all TOs except standard Windows objects.

Accessing web elements through DOM

Although UFT provides a rich interface that encapsulates the most common operations required to manipulate web elements (for example, click, double-click, set, select, and so on), it has some limitations. For instance, UFT does not give us an obvious way to verify the style of the text. In such a case, we will refer to the **Document Object Model** (**DOM**) to get access to the native methods and properties of the elements. Another situation that would justify such usage would be when the performance of the test run is hindered when a huge amount of elements needs to be processed. For example, processing a table with lots of rows and columns through UFT's `WebTable` interface takes much longer than accessing these same elements through DOM. In this recipe, we will see how to get the style of an element and how to get a collection of elements with a particular HTML tag.

How to do it...

Proceed with the following steps:

1. First, we will get a reference to the `document` object:

   ```
   Dim document

   Set document = Browser("title:=.*Advanced
     QTP.*").Page("title:=.+").Object
   ```

   The `InternetExplorer.Application` COM object is an alternative to the previous code to get the document object:

   ```
   Dim IE

   Set IE = CreateObject("InternetExplorer.Application")

   IE.Navigate "http://www.advancedqtp.com"

   Set document = IE.Document
   ```

2. Let us see how we can get the style of an element.

   The style of an element is actually an object that contains different attributes. First, we will get a reference to a specific object:

   ```
   Dim searchBox

   Set searchBox = document.getElementByName("s")
   ```

We will then be able to access the style attributes:

```
Dim searchBox

Print searchBox.style.backgroundColor
Print searchBox.style.fontSize
Print searchBox.style.fontFamily
```

3. Next, let's see how we can get a collection of elements with a particular HTML tag:

   Here we will see how to get a collection of elements through DOM instead of using UFT's `ChildObjects` method:

   ```
   Dim allImages

   Set allImages = document.getElementsByTagName("img")
   ```

   It is then possible to loop through the individual elements and perform different verifications and operations. Keep in mind that these are native HTML objects and not UFT TOs.

How it works...

When we work through DOM, it is like stepping out of UFT. When we get a reference to the document, all native methods and properties are available to us. In general, working through DOM should be faster than working through the UFT interface. However, utilities provided by UFT, such as the Object Repository, serve as a database to store the descriptions of the objects that appear in AUT.

See also

Refer *QTP Descriptive Programming Unplugged, KnowledgeInbox,* by Anshoo Arora and Tarun Lalwani

3
Testing XML and Database

In this chapter, we will cover the following recipes:

- ▶ Establishing and closing a database connection
- ▶ Using SQL queries programmatically
- ▶ Using a database checkpoint
- ▶ Using an XML checkpoint

Introduction

This chapter provides some basic recipes to handle **Database** (**DB**) and XML testing within UFT.

It provides essential support for data connectivity to both external databases and **Extensible Markup Language** (**XML**) file formats within the function library.

This chapter does not detail the API test functionality that was recently introduced within Unified Functional Tester Version 12 as part of the integration with the Service Test product line, which provides native support and additional functionality around DB and XML within the Standard Activities Toolbox.

Establishing and closing a database connection

In this recipe, we will show how to establish a DB connection using VBScript code. We will build a simple custom class, `DB_Handler` that will be instantiated using a global scope variable, `oDBHandler`. This global object will serve as the basis for all our DB operations.

Getting ready

From the **File** menu, navigate to **New** | **Function Library...** or use the *Alt + Shift + N* shortcut. Name the new function library `DB_Func.vbs`.

How to do it...

The following code handles creating, opening, and closing a DB connection using `ADODB`:

```
Const C_ADODB_OBJ = "ADODB.Connection"
Dim oDBHandler

Function createDBHandler(p, ds, ic, uid, pwd)
    On error resume next
    Set oDBHandler=new DB_Handler

    call oDBHandler.Init(p, ds, ic, uid, pwd)

    createDBHandler=eval("err.number=0")
End Function

Class DB_Handler
    private m_oDBConnection
    Public Provider
    Public DataSource
    Public InitialCatalog
    Public Username
    Public Password

    Function Init()
        With me
            .Provider=p
            .DataSource=ds
            .InitialCatalog=ic
            .Username=uid
```

```
                .Password=pwd
            End With
      End Function

      Function openDBConnection()
            m_oDBConnection.open(createConnectionString())
      End function

      Function closeDBConnection()
            m_oDBConnection.close()
      End Function

      Function createConnectionString()
            createConnectionString = "Provider="&Provider& _
                              ";Data Source="&DataSource& _
                              ";Initial
                                Catalog="&InitialCatalog& _
                              ";uid="&myUserName&";pwd="&Password
      End Function

      Function createDBConnection()
            If not lcase(typename(m_oDBConnection)) =
              lcase(C_ADODB_OBJ) Then
                Set m_oDBConnection = CreateObject(C_ADODB_OBJ)
            End If
      End Function
      Function disposeDBConnection()
            closeDBConnection()
            Set m_oDBConnection = nothing
      End Function

      Private Sub Class_Initialize()
            createDBConnection()
      End Sub
      Private Sub Class_Terminate()
            disposeDBConnection()
      End Sub
   End Class
```

Now, we can run Action1 with the following lines of code:

```
dim p, ds, ic, uid, pwd

p="{SQL Server}"
```

```
ds="yourServername"
ic="yourDatabasename"
uid="yourUsername"
pwd="yourPassword"

if not createDBHandler(p, ds, ic, uid, pwd) then
    Reporter.ReportEvent micFail, "DB Init", "Failed to create a
      DB Handler instance."
    exittest
end if

'Open the connection
oDBHandler.openDBConnection()

'Here goes code to query the DB (see recipe Using SQL queries
  programmatically)
'...
'...

'Close the connection
oDBHandler.closeDBConnection()

'Dispose the DB Handler
set oDBHandler=nothing
```

How it works...

We first declare the variables that we need to define our connection string. The `Provider` connection string tells `ADODB` the database type we intend to use (Access, SQL Server, Oracle, and so on). `DataSource` is the server or path on which our DB is located. `InitialCatalog` is the DB we wish to use upon connecting to the server. `Username` and `Password` are, of course, the credentials with which we log in to the DB.

We then call the `createDBHandler(p, ds, ic, uid, pwd)` method that serves as our constructor for the `DB_Handler` class. We pass the arguments listed here, and the method takes care of creating a new instance and initializing it with our parameters by calling the class member function `init(p, ds, ic, uid, pwd)`. If an error occurs, then the method returns `false` (eval="err.number=0" would evaluate to `false`), and the code would exit the test after reporting the event to the test results.

With our object already initialized, we can proceed to call its `openDBConnection()` function, perform the SQL queries we need, and at the end take care of calling `closeDBConnection()`. At the end, we dispose of our `DBHandler` object.

Using SQL queries programmatically

In the previous recipe, we discussed how to use a UFT DB checkpoint. Here, we will show you how to execute a SQL statement using VBScript code.

Getting ready

We will use the function library `DB_Func.vbs` as in the previous recipe *Establishing and closing a database connection*.

How to do it...

In our custom class `DB_Handler`, we will add a new private `m_oRecordset` field to hold the results of our query and a new method `executeSQLQuery(SQLQuery)`, which, of course, accepts a string with a valid SQL query as the argument:

```
Private m_oRecordset

function executeSQLQuery(SQLQuery)
    Set m_oRecordset = m_oDBConnection.Execute(SQLQuery)
End Function
```

Additionally, in our `Action1` datasheet, we would call the `executeSQLQuery(SQLQuery)` method by passing our SQL string as the argument:

```
call oDBHandler.executeSQLQuery(SQLQuery)
```

As mentioned earlier, the method would store the returned `Recordset` in the `m_oRecordset` field. Then, we will be able to perform operations with these data, such as making comparison between the expected and actual results.

How it works...

With our `oDBHandler` object already initialized and having an open DB connection, as shown in the previous recipe, we call the `executeSQLQuery` member function passing our SQL query string as the parameter. Inside the `m_oRecordset` method, member field is assigned the result of the `Execute` method of the `ADODB.Connection` object.

Using a database checkpoint

We have seen in the previous recipes how to connect and perform SQL queries programmatically. This knowledge is essential because it can give us more flexibility as to how to access our DB and how to process the retrieved data. However, UFT provides an in-built feature to perform DB checkpoints, which can be very useful especially when the person implementing the automated tests is less skilled in coding.

Getting ready

We will use the `flight32.mdb` file supplied with the Flight application, which we used in *Chapter 1, Data-driven Tests*. Make sure that the Microsoft Query application is installed on your machine.

How to do it...

Proceed with the following steps:

1. From the UFT menu, navigate to **Design | Checkpoint | Database Checkpoint**:

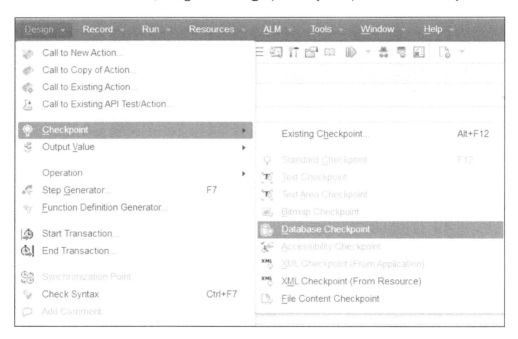

2. Now, the **Database Query Wizard** dialog will open:

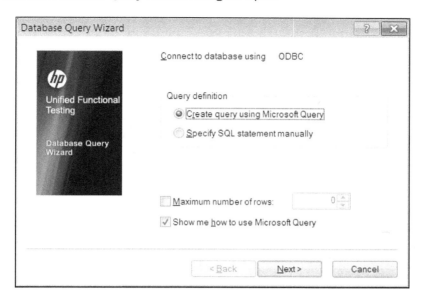

3. Now, in the **Database Query Wizard** dialog, we can choose to define our SQL statement using Microsoft Query, or we can do so manually. If we select the first option, **Create query using Microsoft Query**, and leave the **Show me how to use Microsoft Query** checkbox marked, the following dialog will appear:

4. After closing the **Instructions for Microsoft Query** dialog, the **Microsoft Query** application will open:

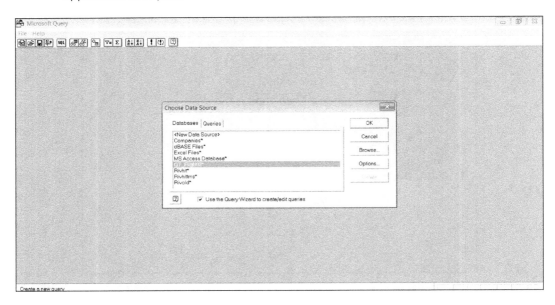

5. From the **Choose Data Source** dialog, we will select **QT_Flight32***:

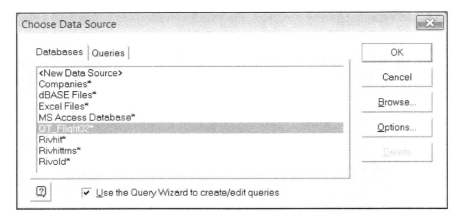

6. Next, the **Query Wizard - Choose Columns** window will open:

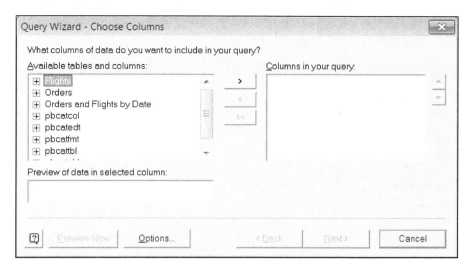

7. For our sample query, we will select all columns from the Flights table. You can opt to use fewer columns if you wish. Each column must be selected, and then the **>** button should be clicked on to include it in the **Columns in your query** list to the right of the window. The following screenshot shows an intermediate state of both lists (**Seats_Available** and the selected columns):

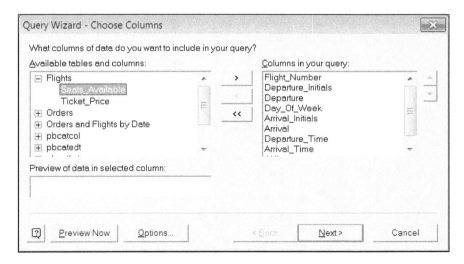

8. After finishing the selection of columns, we click on **Next**, and the next step is to build a filter for our query (equivalent to the WHERE statement in a SQL query). For example, we will select flights which depart on Sundays, as shown in the following screenshot:

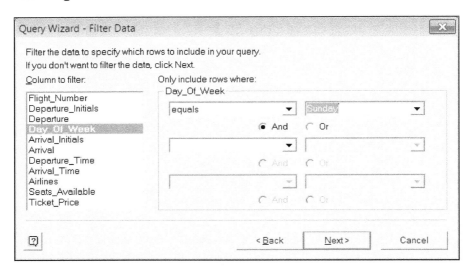

9. After clicking on **Next**, we will be able to define how we wish to sort the data. We will choose to sort the data according to the Departure column in ascending order, as shown:

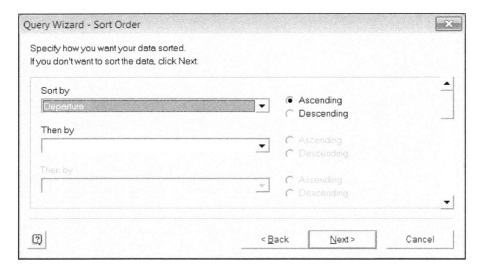

10. Now, clicking on **Next** will lead to the last screen **Query Wizard - Finish** dialog:

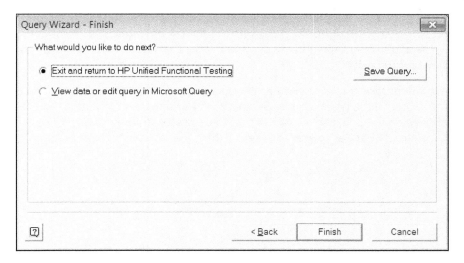

11. You can now save the query before exiting the process, view the data, or edit the query. We will stick to the default action and exit the process to return to UFT, in which the **Database Checkpoint Properties** dialog will open:

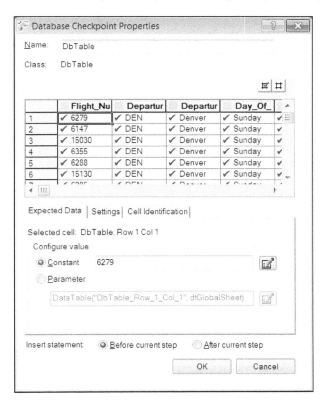

In the grid at the top of the preceding screenshot, we can see the numbered records of the `Flights` DB table, with the data in each cell for each of the columns we selected. Below the grid, we see three tabs: **Expected Data**, **Settings**, and **Cell Identification**.

12. **Expected Data** can be **Constant** (the default option) or **Parameter**. We can configure the source of the parameter by selecting the **Parameter** radio button, and then clicking on the edit icon to the right. The **Parameter Options** dialog will open. Please note that **Parameter** will refer to the currently selected cell in the grid:

13. We can now select whether the value will be taken from the DataTable (either global or local), Environment, or a random number in the case of a DB checkpoint. It is also possible to define a parameter as a regular expression.

14. The **Settings** tab enables us to define whether the data verification will be done as a simple text or numeric comparison, or as a numeric range. We can also indicate whether we require an exact match, whether spaces should be ignored, and whether the letter case should be matched, as shown in the following screenshot:

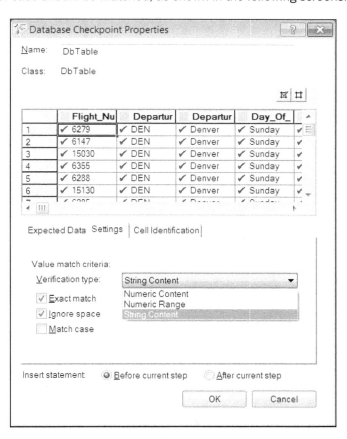

15. Finally, in the **Cell Identification** tab, we can define how we wish to identify our cells. For the rows, it is possible to use its number or key columns, and use **Value match criteria** defined in the **Settings** tab to identify a cell. For the columns, it is possible to use the column position or name, as shown:

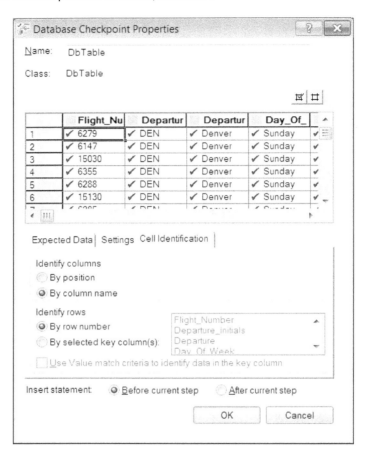

16. After finishing the definition of our checkpoint properties, we select whether we want the resulting statement to appear before or after the current step. In our case, it does not matter, so we will leave the default value (**Before current step**) as it is, and click on **OK**. The resulting code is:

```
DbTable("DbTable").Check CheckPoint("DbTable")
```

17. Our Object Repository now includes `DbTable` as **Test Object** and a `DbTable` checkpoint object, as in the following screenshot:

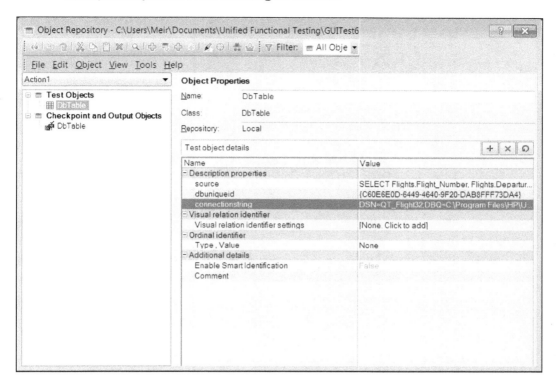

The `DbTable` TO will show that three description properties are used:

- `source`: This contains the SQL query we generated using the Microsoft Query Wizard.

- `dbuniqueid`: This contains a **Globally Unique Identifier** (**GUID**).

- `connectionstring`: This contains the connection string used to connect to the DB. We would use this to connect through raw VBScript code.

The `DbTable` checkpoint will show the settings, as we defined earlier in the **Database Checkpoint Properties** dialog:

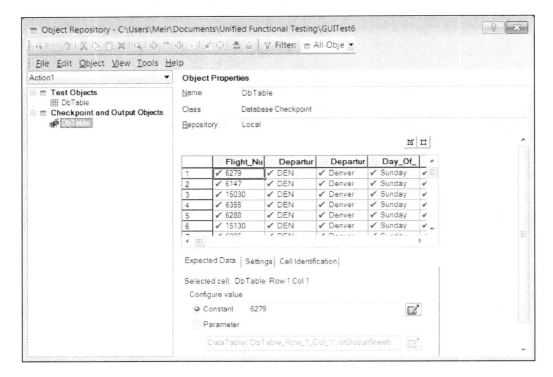

How it works...

When invoking the Datatable, using the `DbTable.check` method with the DB checkpoint object, a connection is established using the connection string. Then, the data will be retrieved using the SQL query we defined, and each cell is compared to its identified counterpart using the value match criteria. Running the previous code will result in a results report, as follows:

Using an XML checkpoint

Since the early 1990s XML files have been widely used for data transfer between application modules and even between different systems. An XML file may contain, for instance, the results of a billing record for a cellular phone customer. In such a case, it may be of high value to be able to have preset expected results and be able to compare actual XML files with these.

How to do it...

Proceed with the following steps:

1. From the UFT menu navigate to **Design | Checkpoint | XML Checkpoint (From Resource)**, which will open the dialog by the same title:

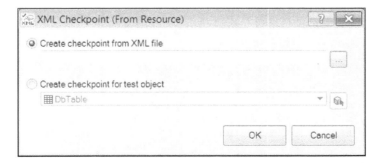

2. Click on the Browse button and select a file from the **Open XML File** dialog. In our example, we will be using a sample XML given by Microsoft with the following contents:

```
<?xml version="1.0"?>
<catalog>
   <book id="bk101">
      <author>Gambardella, Matthew</author>
      <title>XML Developer's Guide</title>
      <genre>Computer</genre>
      <price>44.95</price>
      <publish_date>2000-10-01</publish_date>
      <description>An in-depth look at creating applications
         with XML.</description>
   </book>
   <book id="bk102">
      <author>Ralls, Kim</author>
      <title>Midnight Rain</title>
      <genre>Fantasy</genre>
      <price>5.95</price>
      <publish_date>2000-12-16</publish_date>
      <description>A former architect battles corporate
         zombies, an evil sorceress, and her own childhood to
         become queen of the world.</description>
   </book>
   <book id="bk103">
      <author>Lucas, George</author>
      <title>The Force Awakens</title>
      <genre>Sci-Fi</genre>
      <price>11.78</price>
      <publish_date>2015-12-18</publish_date>
      <description> Set approximately 30 years after the
         defeat of the Empire and the demise of Darth Vader,
         the plot follows a trio of young leads, along with
         characters from the previous installments.</description>
   </book>
   <book id="bk104">
      <author>Wright, Jonathon</author>
      <title>Experiences of Test Automation</title>
      <genre>Computer</genre>
      <price>25.95</price>
      <publish_date>2012-01-09</publish_date>
      <description>Software test automation has moved beyond a
         luxury to become a necessity. Applications and systems
         have grown ever larger and more complex, and manual testing
         simply cannot keep up.</description>
```

```
    </book>
    <book id="bk105">
       <author>Crispin, Lisa</author>
       <title>Agile Testing: A Practical Guide</title>
       <genre>Computer</genre>
       <price>25.95</price>
       <publish_date>2008-12-30</publish_date>
       <description> Testing is a key component of agile
         development. The widespread adoption of agile methods
         has brought the need for effective testing.</description>
    </book>
    <book id="bk106">
       <author>Graham, Dorothy</author>
       <title>Software Test Automation</title>
       <genre>Computer</genre>
       <price>14.95</price>
       <publish_date>1999-05-28</publish_date>
       <description> This book describes how to build and implement
         an automated testing regime for software development.
         It presents a detailed account of the principles of
         automated testing.</description>
    </book>
    <book id="bk107">
       <author>Hendrickson, Elisabeth</author>
       <title>Explore It!</title>
       <genre>Computer</genre>
       <price>14.95</price>
       <publish_date>2013-03-03</publish_date>
       <description> Uncover surprises, risks, and potentially
         serious bugs with exploratory testing. Rather than
         designing all tests in advance, explorers design and
         execute small, rapid experiments.</description>
    </book>
    <book id="bk108">
       <author>Adzic, Gojko</author>
       <title>Specification by Example</title>
       <genre>Computer</genre>
       <price>24.95</price>
       <publish_date>2011-05-06</publish_date>
       <description> Specification by Example is an emerging
         practice for creating software based on realistic examples,
         bridging the communication gap between business
         stakeholders and the dev teams building the software.
         </description>
    </book>
```

```
<book id="bk109">
   <author>Whittaker, James</author>
   <title>How Google Tests Software</title>
   <genre>Computer</genre>
   <price>16.95</price>
   <publish_date>2012-03-23</publish_date>
   <description> Do you need to get it right, too? Then, learn
     from Google.</description>
</book>
<book id="bk110">
   <author>O'Brien, Tim</author>
   <title>Microsoft .NET: The Programming Bible</title>
   <genre>Computer</genre>
   <price>36.95</price>
   <publish_date>2000-12-09</publish_date>
   <description>Microsoft's .NET initiative is explored in
     detail in this deep programmer reference.</description>
</book>
<book id="bk111">
   <author>O'Brien, Tim</author>
   <title>MSXML3: A Comprehensive Guide</title>
   <genre>Computer</genre>
   <price>36.95</price>
   <publish_date>2000-12-01</publish_date>
   <description>The Microsoft MSXML3 parser is covered in
     detail, with attention to XML DOM interfaces, XSLT
     processing, SAX and more.</description>
</book>
<book id="bk112">
   <author>Galos, Mike</author>
   <title>Visual Studio 7: A Comprehensive Guide</title>
   <genre>Computer</genre>
   <price>49.95</price>
   <publish_date>2001-04-16</publish_date>
   <description>Microsoft Visual Studio 7 is explored in
     depth, looking at how Visual Basic, Visual C++, C#,
     and ASP+ are integrated into a comprehensive development
     environment.</description>
</book>
</catalog>
```

3. At the end, click on **OK**. The **XML Checkpoint Properties** dialog will appear, as shown:

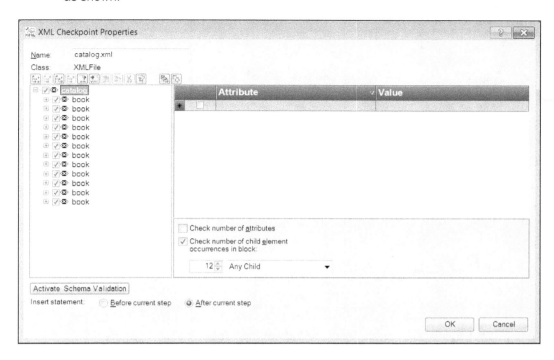

Now, for each node we will be able to define whether we wish to:

❑   Check the number of attributes it has (if any).

❑   Check the number of child elements.

❑   Limit our verification to a particular type of child (relevant when more than a single type is present). In our example, under the **catalog** root node, we only have **book** nodes so it does not make any difference.

When traversing the hierarchy we can view the specific values of nodes, as shown:

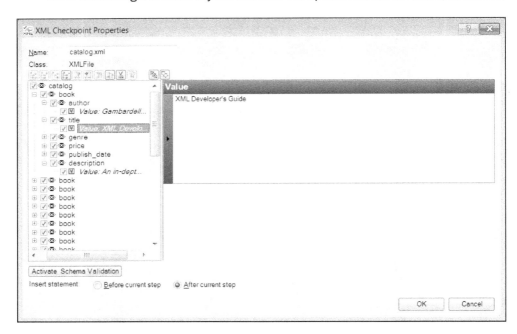

We can also click on the **Activate Schema Validation** button to validate the integrity of the XML document with regards to a schema (XSD), either referenced in the document or an external one:

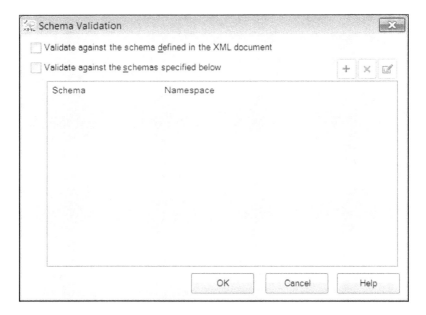

In case our, XML is expected to be based on such a schema, this would give us a comprehensive checkpoint, which not only verifies the contents of the XML document but also its structure.

4. At the end of the definitions, we click on **OK**, and the following statement is inserted in `Action`:

```
XMLFile("catalog.xml").Check CheckPoint("catalog.xml")
```

In addition, our Object Repository now includes `XMLFile` as TO and a `CheckPoint` object of `XMLFile`. The `XMLFile` TO carries a single description property, that is, its filename, which stores its path. Of course, as with other TOs, it is possible to parameterize this property. In a similar fashion, as with the `DbTable` checkpoint, the `CheckPoint` object of `XMLFile` will have the properties as we defined in the **XML Checkpoint Properties** dialog previously.

How it works...

When invoking the `Check` method of `XMLFile` with the XML `CheckPoint` object, the target file is opened and checked against the data stored as expected results. Running the command yields a results report, as follows (here we have deliberately changed one value in the XML file to make the checkpoint fail):

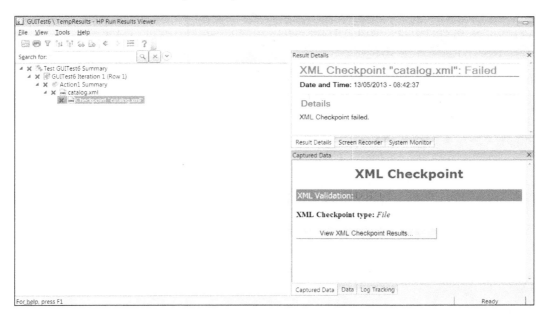

If prompted to allow ActiveX Add-In, then approve in order to see **Captured Data**. Clicking on the **View XML Checkpoint Results** button in that pane will open a window titled **XML Checkpoint Results**:

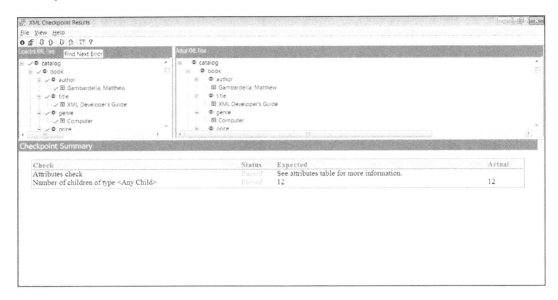

We see that for each node there is a checkpoint summary giving details about the checks that were performed. As the tooltip shows, we can browse through our results very efficiently to drill-down and examine the failures. Clicking on the icon to find the next error will lead us to the node in which UFT found a discrepancy between the expected and actual data:

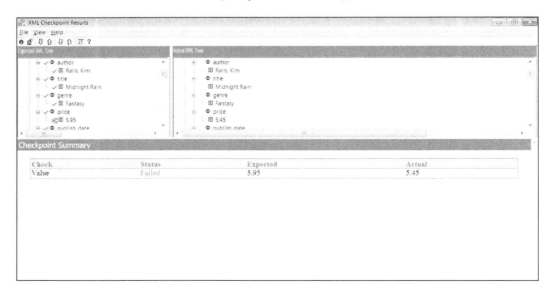

4
Method Overriding

In this chapter, we will cover the following recipes:

- ▶ Overriding a Test Object method
- ▶ Registering a method to all classes
- ▶ Using method overriding to support object subtypes
- ▶ Adding a new method to a class

Introduction

Method overriding is a feature of object-oriented programming languages such as C++, C#, and Java. It enables us to adopt a method or property inherited from a base class in order to address specific requirements of a class. In certain cases, overriding a method is necessary; for example, when a method in the base class is defined as abstract, or when an interface is implemented.

In UFT, the need to override a method may arise. The reasons can be diverse, from handling a customized version of a common control, to enriching the basic function, or even integrating the TO methods with an exception handling mechanism. As we will see in this chapter, it is also possible to add methods to a TO(s).

Overriding a Test Object method

In this recipe, we will see how to write a new implementation of a method for a TO.

Getting ready

From the **File** menu, navigate to **New | Function Library...** or use the *Alt + Shift + N* shortcut. Name the new function library as `FR_RegFunc.vbs`.

How to do it...

As always, with programming, the task needs to be addressed in an orderly fashion. Therefore, there is a series of implementation steps to follow:

1. Analyze the requirement, which means ask questions. For example:
   - What are the missing functions?
   - To which object class is it relevant?
2. Design the solution.
3. Code the function.
4. Test the function.
5. Register the function to the required object class.

In the following example, we will write a function in `FR_RegFunc.vbs` that overrides the `WinEdit_Set` method. The new method will try to set the field, and if an error occurs, it will check if there is a modal pop-up message that has opened in the Flight Reservation application (refer to *Chapter 1, Data-driven Test*). If it has opened, the method will close it and the flow may continue.

```
'If there is a problem when trying to set a WinEdit control with
  text, then the function checks whether a modal popup is open and
  closes it
Function FR_WinEdit_Set(obj, text)
    On error resume next
    reporter.Filter = rfDisableAll 'Disable automatic reporting
    obj.set text
    reporter.Filter = rfEnableAll 'Enable automatic reporting
    'If the operation failed
    If err.number <> 0  Then
```

```
'Report a warning so the test does not fail
reporter.ReportEvent micWarning, "Set on " &
  obj.GetTOProperty("name"), "Tried to set WinEdit with
  value " & text & vbNewLine & _
    err.number & ": " & err.description
'An error was found, check if a popup dialog is open
If obj.GetTOProperty("parent").
  Dialog("ispopupwindow:=true").exist(0) Then
    'Report and Close popup
    Reporter.ReportEvent micDone, "Popup dialog found",
      "Closing dialog"
    obj.GetTOProperty("parent").Dialog("ispopupwindow:=true").
      WinButton("text:=OK").click
    'TODO: Decide which implementation is more suitable
    '1. We can try to set the field again
    '2. Return the control to the calling Action (as we do
        here)
    '3. Other
  End If
 End If
End Function
```

We then run `Action1` with the following lines of code:

```
'Register the overriding method
RegisterUserFunc "WinEdit", "Set", "FR_WinEdit_Set"
'Try to set the Agent Name field in the FR Login dialog
Dialog("Login").WinEdit("Agent Name").Set "mercury"
'Unregister the overriding method
UnregisterUserFunc "WinEdit", "Set"
```

It is important to note that `RegisterUserFunc` is used during runtime to load the custom function for native method mappings. However, it is also possible to do this while designing via the UFT GUI, by navigating to **Design | Function Definition Generator** from the menu. This will provide you with autocomplete/intellisense in your test. Of course, the function library containing the custom functions must be available in the test's resources.

How it works...

The implemented custom method takes two arguments, namely, `obj` and `text`. The first is for the TO, `WinEdit` and the second is for the text to be entered. First, to obtain full control over the flow, we disable VBScript's native runtime error handling mechanism with `On Error Resume Next`. Second, to avoid the test being marked as failed automatically, we disable UFT's automatic event reporting by assigning `Reporter.Filter = rfDisableAll` to the `Filter` property of the `Reporter` object. Next, we set the value and restore `Filter` to its default value `Reporter.Filter = rfEnableAll`.

Mode	Description
0 or `rfEnableAll`	This is the default value. All reported events are displayed in the run results.
1 or `rfEnableErrorsAndWarnings`	This mode displays events with a warning or failed status in the run results.
2 or `rfEnableErrorsOnly`	This mode displays events with a failed status in the run results.
3 or `rfDisableAll`	This mode does not display any events in the run results.

In the following example, we will demonstrate all `Filter` properties of the `Reporter` object combinations from the preceding table:

```
Reporter.ReportEvent micPass, "Step 1", "Passed"
Reporter.ReportEvent micFail, "Step 2", "Failed"

'Disable all the Results
Reporter.Filter = rfDisableAll
Reporter.ReportEvent micPass, "Step 3", "Passed"
Reporter.ReportEvent micFail, "Step 4", "Failed"

'Enable Result Display
Reporter.Filter = rfEnableAll
Reporter.ReportEvent micWarning, "Step 5", "Warning"

'Enable only Errors and Warnings
Reporter.Filter = rfEnableErrorsAndWarnings
Reporter.ReportEvent micPass, "Step 6", "Passed"
Reporter.ReportEvent micFail, "Step 7", "Failed"
Reporter.ReportEvent micWarning, "Step 8", "Warning"
```

If an error of any kind occurs, it will be caught by the `If err.number <> 0 Then` clause. Then, our custom exception handling will be executed. In the preceding example, we report all types of warnings, but a specific implementation may select one type, depending on the requirements. For instance, the error may occur under controlled conditions (such as `negative test(s)`), and hence, our implementation should be more complex to cover such situations. In any case, it is recommended to leave the custom function as simple as possible.

The next step is to check if the parent container (window or dialog) has a child (owned) pop-up dialog open, which, it is reasonable to assume, is modal and therefore obstructs the target `WinEdit`, causing the error. If this is the case, then we report our findings and click on `OK` on the pop-up dialog `WinButton`.

There's more...

At this stage one may ask, what now? How do we decide on the correct implementation? As mentioned earlier, this depends on the requirements. For example, if the previous custom method is meant to be a recovery scenario, then we might want to add the following code to close the pop-up code that ensures `WinEdit` is actually assigned the text passed to the function. In such a case, our function code would change to:

```
'Continued...
obj.GetTOProperty("parent").Dialog("ispopupwindow:=true").
  WinButton("text:=OK").click
obj.Set text
```

It is not recommended to use a recursion, for example, with the following:

```
Call FR_WinEdit_Set(obj, text)
```

However, it is possible to shorten the syntax:

```
obj.set text
```

There are two limitations that must be taken into account when using the `RegisterUserFunc`:

- ▸ Number of arguments
- ▸ Interoperability of registered functions

Number of function arguments

When defining a function that overrides a method, it must have the same signature. This means that the overriding function cannot have a number of arguments different from the original method that is overridden. A workaround is to have one of the mandatory arguments sent as an array or, even better, as a dictionary. This way, you can have a customized version of the method that, in practice, is able to operate with a different number of arguments. It is even possible to design it in such a way that the custom method will treat items of the array or dictionary as optional.

Interoperability of registered functions

When a registered function includes a call to another registered function, be careful and use the correct syntax. To call a registered function so that no changes to existing calls should be carried out, we usually put a statement such as:

```
call obj.[native method]([arg1], [...], [argn])
```

To avoid a VBScript runtime error (`Type Mismatch`) during your run session, when a call from one overriding method to another is required, the limitations can be overcome by coding the call as follows:

```
call [custom method](obj, [arg1], [...], [argn])
```

See also

The following articles on `www.advancedqtp.com` also discuss `RegisterUserFunc` in depth:

- An article by Yaron Assa at `http://www.advancedqtp.com/a-fresh-look-on-registeruserfunc`

- An article by Meir Bar-Tal at `http://www.advancedqtp.com/override-the-object-exist-property`

- An article by Meir Bar-Tal `http://www.advancedqtp.com/limitations-of-registeruserfunc`

Registering a method to all classes

In some cases, we may need to customize a method that is common to all TO classes, or at least to all references to a particular environment, such as the Web or Java. For example, suppose we need to customize the `Click` method and register all Web TO classes. To write a statement for each class is quite tedious, and it may be an error-prone practice. For example:

```
RegisterUserFunc "WebEdit", "Click", "AQTP_Click"
RegisterUserFunc "WebButton", "Click", "AQTP_Click"
RegisterUserFunc "WebRadiobutton", "Click", "AQTP_Click"
```

If the new implemented method needs to be registered to all classes of all environments, then it becomes impractical and undesirable to maintain this via code. We can manage such custom function registrations better by using a data-driven approach.

Getting ready

You can use the `FR_RegFunc.vbs` function library as in the *Overriding a Test Object method* recipe.

How to do it...

Perform the following steps:

1. In the function library, we will write the following code:

```
Dim QTP_TO_ENVS

Function LoadTOEnvironments()
        Set QTP_TO_ENVS = CreateObject("Scripting.Dictionary")
        QTP_TO_ENVS("Java") =       Array(    "JavaButton", _
                                    "JavaCalendar", _
                                    "JavaCheckBox", _
                                    "JavaDialog", _
                                    "JavaEdit", _
                                    "JavaExpandBar", _
                                    "JavaInternalFrame", _
                                    "JavaLink", _
                                    "JavaList", _
                                    "JavaMenu", _
                                    "JavaObject", _
                                    "JavaRadioButton", _
                                    "JavaSlider", _
                                    "JavaSpin", _
                                    "JavaStaticText", _
                                    "JavaTab", _
                                    "JavaTable", _
                                    "JavaToolbar", _
                                    "JavaTree", _
                                    "JavaWindow")
        QTP_TO_ENVS("Web") =        Array(    "Browser", _
                                    "Frame", _
                                    "Image", _
                                    "Link", _
                                    "Page", _
                                    "ViewLink", _
                                    "WebArea", _
                                    "WebButton", _
                                    "WebCheckBox", _
                                    "WebEdit", _
                                    "WebElement", _
                                    "WebFile", _
                                    "WebList", _
```

```
                                              "WebRadioGroup", _
                                              "WebTable", _
                                              "WebXML")

        QTP_TO_ENVS("StdWin") =       Array(   "Desktop", _
                                              "Dialog", _
                                              "Static", _
                                              "SystemUtil", _
                                              "WinButton", _
                                              "WinCheckBox", _
                                              "WinComboBox", _
                                              "Window", _
                                              "WinEdit", _
                                              "WinEditor", _
                                              "WinList", _
                                              "WinListView", _
                                              "WinMenu", _
                                              "WinObject", _
                                              "WinRadioButton", _
                                              "WinScrollBar", _
                                              "WinSpin", _
                                              "WinStatusBar", _
                                              "WinTab", _
                                              "WinToolbar", _
                                              "WinTreeView")
End function

Public Function ValidateTOClasses(ByVal strAddIn, ByRef
  arrTOClasses)
    If IsArray(arrTOClasses) Then
        If UBound(arrTOClasses) = -1 Then
            'Empty Array, so assign default (all)
            arrTOClasses = QTP_TO_ENVS(strAddIn)
        End If
    Else
        'Not an Array, so assign default (all)
        arrTOClasses = QTP_TO_ENVS(strAddIn)
    End If
End Function


Function RegisterUserFuncEx(ByVal strAddIn, ByVal
  arrTOClasses, ByVal strOverriddenMethod, ByVal
  strNewMethod)
```

```
        Dim ix

        Call ValidateTOClasses(strAddIn, arrTOClasses)

        If IsEmpty(strOverriddenMethod) Or
          Trim(strOverriddenMethod) = "" Then
          strOverriddenMethod = strNewMethod

        For ix = 0 To UBound(arrTOClasses)
            If Left(arrTOClasses(ix), 1) <> "-" Then
                Call RegisterUserFunction(arrTOClasses(ix),
                  strOverriddenMethod, strNewMethod)
            Else
                Print "Char '-' found at left position 1.
                  Skipped registration of function" &
                  strNewMethod & " to method " &
                  strOverriddenMethod & " in class " &
                  strTOClass
            End If
        Next
End Function


Function UnregisterUserFuncEx(ByVal strAddIn, ByVal
  arrTOClasses, ByVal strOverriddenMethod)
    Dim ix

    Call ValidateTOClasses(strAddIn, arrTOClasses)

    If IsEmpty(strOverriddenMethod) Or
      Trim(strOverriddenMethod) = "" Then
      strOverriddenMethod = strNewMethod

    For ix = 0 To UBound(arrTOClasses)
        If Left(arrTOClasses(ix), 1) <> "-" Then
            Call UnregisterUserFunc(arrTOClasses(ix),
              strOverriddenMethod)
        Else
            Print "Char '-' found at left position 1.
              Skipped unregistering method " &
              strOverriddenMethod & " in class " &
              strTOClass
        End If
    Next
End function
```

We will also add a custom function to override the `Click` method:

```
Function FR_Click(obj)
    Print "This is my custom Click function"

    obj.click
End Function
```

2. In `Action`, write the following code:

```
'Load the global dictionary with each environment's classes
call LoadTOEnvironments()
'Register the overriding method to all classes in StdWin env
call RegisterUserFuncEx("StdWin", array(), "click", "FR_Click")
'Register the overriding method to the WinEdit class
RegisterUserFunc "WinEdit", "Set", "FR_WinEdit_Set"
'Try to set the Agent Name field in the FR Login dialog
Dialog("Login").WinEdit("Agent Name").Set "mercury"
'Unregister the overriding method
UnregisterUserFunc "WinEdit", "Set"
call UnregisterUserFuncEx("StdWin", array(), "click")
```

In the output pane, you will notice that the printed script is **This is my custom Click function**, which is a line we added in our custom version of the `Click` method.

How it works...

Here, we will skip the parts of the code already explained in the *Overriding a Test Object method* recipe.

First, we call the `LoadTOEnvironments` function to get a dictionary object assigned to our `QTP_TO_ENVS` global variable, which will store for us a key for each environment we defined, each pointing to an array with a list of all the classes within that environment.

Then, we call the `RegisterUserFuncEx` function (our custom version of `RegisterUserFunc`) seeking to register the `FR_Click` function in the `Click` method for all classes (hence the empty array is passed) within the `StdWin` environment.

The `ValidateTOClasses` function checks whether the argument passed to the `RegisterUserFuncEx` function is an array or an empty array. In such a case, the function registers the custom method to all classes listed in the `QTP_TO_ENVS(strAddIn)` array. If a hyphen (-) is added to the left of the class name, then the method will not be registered to that particular class (and eventually, of course, will not be unregistered at all).

The flow is otherwise the same as in the previous recipe, but when the OK button of the pop-up dialog is clicked, UFT reroutes the call to our registered FR_Click function, and hence, the custom output (as mentioned in the previous section). In a way, we can say that our custom function is actually a delegate of the native method.

At the end of the script, we unregister the custom function from all classes in the environment (in this case, StdWin).

Using method overriding to support object subtypes

In some cases, we may need to implement different versions of the same native method to reflect different subtypes of a particular control class. To achieve this, we can use method overriding with RegisterUserFunc and reroute our test flow dynamically. For example, suppose that **Application Under Test** (**AUT**) uses different types of input controls, such as a password (encrypted) field, specially formatted fields for ID, date, and email, or even just for text, as opposed to numeric only data. In such cases, we might wish to use specific code to validate the input data or even (in a very advanced implementation) to generate it randomly.

Let us take, for example, two input fields (WebEdit) having different class HTML native attributes. We will write a custom version of the WebEdit_Set method (actually a delegate) that will reroute the function to execute a specific piece of code for the given element class.

Getting ready

From the **File** menu, navigate to **New** | **Function Library** or use the *Alt + Shift + N* shortcut. Name the new function library as Web_RegFunc.vbs.

In an external HTML editor, create an HTML file and name it WebEdit_Subtype.html. Write the following HTML code and save the file:

```html
<html>
  <head>
    <title>AdvancedQTP - Overriding TO Methods Example
    </title>
  </head>
  <body>
    <div><span role="label">Username:</span><input class="normal"
      type="text" name="username"></input></div>
    <div><span role="label">Password:</span><input class="pwd"
      type="password" name="password"></input></div>
    <div><span role="label">Email:</span><input class="normal"
      type="text" name="email"></input></div>
```

```
      <div><span role="label">Tel:</span><input class="not_defined"
        type="text" name="tel"></input></div>
  </body>
  <footer>
  </footer>
</html>
```

Open the file in Internet Explorer and add the four input fields to the local OR. At the end of every stage, do save the test.

How to do it...

Perform the following steps:

1. In the function library, we will write the following code:

```
Function WebEdit_SetEx(obj, str)
    'Reroute the flow based on the obj class
    Select case lcase(obj.GetTOProperty("class"))
        Case "normal"
            print "Regular input"
            obj.set str
        Case "pwd", "enc"
            print "Password input"
            obj.SetSecure
        case else
            print "N/A - Assuming regular input"
            obj.set str
    End Select
End Function
```

2. In Action, we will write our code as usual:

```
RegisterUserFunc "WebEdit", "Set", "WebEdit_SetEx"

with Browser("AdvancedQTP - Overriding").Page("AdvancedQTP
  - Overriding")
    .WebEdit("username").Set "Username"
    .WebEdit("password").Set "Password123"
    .WebEdit("email").Set "email@email.com"
    .WebEdit("tel").Set "(01) 23 456 789"
End with
UnregisterUserFunc "WebEdit", "Set"
```

The flow has rerouted behind the scenes, as explained in the previous recipes. The print log in the **Output** pane, for the four input fields defined in our HTML page, are:

Regular input

Password input

Regular input

N/A - Assuming regular input

How it works...

The WebEdit_Set method was overridden in a different way. While entering the function, the code checks the type of control that invoked the method (the sender) by retrieving the value of its class attribute. According to the result of this inquiry, the function enters the piece of code that was written to handle the specific control subtype. In the case of the Password field, the SetSecure method is invoked instead of Set, to enter the value. In this case, we could have also used the Crypt.Encrypt method with Set, as follows:

```
Function WebEdit_SetEx(obj, str)
    'Reroute the flow based on the obj class
    Select case lcase(obj.GetTOProperty("class"))
        Case "normal"
            print "Regular input"
            obj.set str
        Case "pwd", "enc"
            print "Password input"
            obj.set Crypt.Encrypt(str)
        case else
            print "N/A - Assuming regular input"
            obj.set str
    End Select
End Function
```

There's more...

Another possible application of RegisterUserFunc is to have several versions of a method to support different requirements. The specific custom method to use should be selected during runtime from any Action or function, by calling RegisterUserFunc and UnregisterUserFunc. This may cover cases where we are required to support the following:

► Different versions of the testware framework
► Different configurations of AUT
► The behavior of a TO with context-dependent or dynamically changing behavior

However, if we do change the method registrations during runtime, then we must be extremely cautious, as it may have an impact on the test results. A good practice to meet this risk would be to implement a tracking mechanism, for instance, with a `GlobalDictionary` object (refer to *Chapter 1*, *Data-driven Tests*) from which you would be able to retrieve any class and method, which are the current effective and registered custom methods. Accordingly, it would be possible to validate that the correct method is registered within a given context.

Adding a new method to a class

You can also override an existing TO method and we could actually extend a TO class with new methods. Such custom methods will be registered in the same fashion as those which override the existing ones. For example, if you wish to retrieve the comment property of a TO, use the following code:

```
Print "username: " & Browser("AdvancedQTP -
   Overriding").Page("AdvancedQTP -
   Overriding").WebEdit("username").
   GetTOProperty("miccommentproperty")
```

Instead of writing this every time, the best practice would be to create a new method, which passes in the properties of the TO and returns the retrieved value.

How to do it...

Proceed with the following steps:

1. Open Object Repository in which we previously added the objects from our HTML sample page. Enter the following values (or whichever you choose) to their respective comment fields in the **Properties** pane:

   ```
   WebEdit("username"): Username
   WebEdit("password"): Password123
   WebEdit("email"): email@email.com
   WebEdit("tel"): (01) 23 456 789
   ```

2. We will write the following custom method in our `Web_RegFunc.vbs` function library:

   ```
   Function getTOComment(obj)
        getTOComment = obj.GetTOProperty("miccommentproperty")
   End Function
   ```

3. In our test, we will write the following code:

   ```
   RegisterUserFunc "WebEdit", "Comment", "getTOComment"

   with Browser("AdvancedQTP - Overriding").Page("AdvancedQTP
     - Overriding")
   ```

```
        Print "username: " & .WebEdit("username").Comment
        Print "password: " & .WebEdit("password").Comment
        Print "email: " &.WebEdit("email").Comment
        Print "tel: " &.WebEdit("tel").Comment
    End with

    UnregisterUserFunc "WebEdit", "Comment"
```

The print log in the **Output** pane will show the values as we set them in Object Repository:

username: Username

password: Password123

email: email@email.com

tel: (01) 23 456 789

How it works...

To add a new method or property, we simply map (register) it to a non-existing method, in this case, `Comment`. UFT does not check whether the native TO method exists or not.

The custom function simply retrieves the value of `miccommentproperty` (an undocumented property of TOs), and returns it to the calling function or Action.

During runtime, we call the method or property by the name we decided, in this case, `Comment`, and UFT redirects the call to our `getTOComment` function.

See also

Refer to the following article at `www.advancedqtp.com`, which also discusses this topic in depth:

▶ An article by Meir Bar-Tal at `http://www.advancedqtp.com/add-new-methods-to-objects`

5
Object Identification

In this chapter, we will cover the following recipes:

- ▸ Setting mandatory and assistive properties for a class
- ▸ Using Descriptive Programming inline
- ▸ Using the Description object
- ▸ Using child objects
- ▸ Using native properties for object identification
- ▸ Identifying an object based on its parent

Introduction

This chapter will delve into different aspects of the features provided by UFT to identify GUI **Test Objects** (**TO**). UFT brings along a wide array of add-ins to support different software technologies such as Web, .NET, Java, Delphi, and PowerBuilder. However, despite this diversity that requires a specific add-in implementation for each technology, the basic underlying technology and approach within UFT is the same. In this chapter, we will explain how to make use of this basic approach to tackle the identification of TOs during design and run time. We will also see how to access native properties, which are not supported by UFT out of the box when using `GetROProperty` and `CheckProperty`.

Setting mandatory and assistive properties for a class

In this recipe, we will see how to change the default settings for object identification, which identifies the TO properties that UFT uses in its attempt to achieve unequivocal object identification. After reading this recipe, you will be able to view, analyze, and change the properties UFT uses to identify a TO. You will also acquire a deep understanding of how these properties are used by UFT to achieve object identification.

Getting ready

Before trying this recipe, ensure that the required hooks in the technology adapters, which are defined as add-ins or plug-ins for each of the relevant technologies (Web, .NET, Java, and so on.), are loaded, and that the current test has them defined in its settings.

How to do it...

Proceed with the following steps:

1. From the UFT home page, navigate to **Tools | Object Identification...**. The following dialog will open:

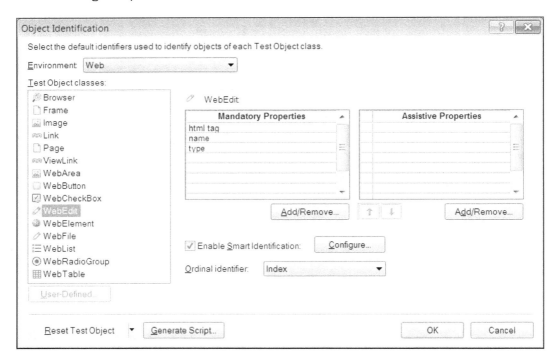

The preceding screenshot shows the dialog after selecting **Web** from the **Environment** listbox and clicking on the `WebEdit` class. We can see that by default, UFT defines three mandatory properties (`html tag`, `name`, and `type`) for this class and has no assistive property.

2. We can change the set of **Mandatory Properties** by clicking on the **Add/Remove** button below the list. The following dialog will open:

We can then mark or unmark any of the listed properties. The properties we choose must have a solid logic behind them: one that will enhance the ability to identify TOs of the particular class correctly. For instance, if an ID is used instead of a name, then we may wish to use only the ID as the identifying property, as it should be unique for each web element.

3. The same procedure can be used for the **Assistive Properties** list by clicking on its **Add/Remove** button. Please note that mandatory and assistive properties are mutually exclusive.

4. Though it is a rarely used feature, it is possible to add custom properties to the default list of properties by using the **New** button, which opens the following dialog:

You must ensure that the property is added by the developer to the objects of this class in the application code.

How it works...

Let us review how object identification is accomplished by UFT and define the basic concepts that underlie in this recipe.

By default, each TO class has two sets of properties defined, namely, mandatory and assistive. UFT mechanism for object identification works as follows:

When you add a TO to OR (for example, by recording a script or by using add object/define new object from the OR menu), the set of mandatory properties is used in full to identify the object, and these will appear in the **Description** properties section on the right-hand pane of the OR. If, however, more than one TO matches the same description as these mandatory properties, UFT will attempt to distinguish between them using the assistive properties. If none are defined for that particular class, then an ordinal identifier, Location or Index, is used. The location identifier refers to the relative position on the client screen, beginning from top to bottom and moving left to right. The index identifier refers to the order in which objects appear in the underlying code. For browser objects, UFT uses creationtime as the ordinal identifier, which is a zero-based index for browser objects, where the first browser gets value zero, the second one gets the value one, and so on.

Finally, if all the attempts fail, UFT will strive to use an identification mechanism called **Smart Identification** (**SI**). This algorithm will try to find the best match for the given description, but it is highly recommended to disable this feature in the project settings and make every possible effort to ensure that all TOs are unequivocally identified. It is possible to disable the use of SI for each run session from the **Run** tab in the **Test Settings** dialog (select this by navigating to **File | Settings**).

There are two reasons for this recommendation. First, the SI mechanism is used as a last resort, so it will start only after UFT fails to identify the object based on the description. Therefore, it might affect the performance of the test. Second, there is no guarantee that the match found by SI is the one you intended to use, and this may lead to unexpected results.

Using Descriptive Programming inline

Apart from storing TOs in OR, UFT supports using **Inline Descriptions** (**ID**), a technique also generally known as **Descriptive Programming** (**DP**). As these descriptions are strings, the technique allows for parameterization, and runtime and dynamic identification of objects using data that was predefined or retrieved from AUT during the run session.

Getting ready

Please ensure that the Internet Explorer application is open on Google.

How to do it...

Suppose that we need to identify an object like one of the links on the Google search engine, such as YouTube, then click on it, and navigate back to Google.

Proceed with the following steps:

1. If we know the values for identification properties (which we can obtain using the UFT Spy), then we can easily write code to accomplish this as follows:

```
with Browser("micclass:=Browser",
   "title:=Google").Page("title:=Google").Link("html
   tag:=A","innertext:=YouTube")
     If .exist(0) Then
          .highlight
          .click
     End If
     Browser("title:=YouTube").Back
End with
```

2. We may be required to parameterize the `innertext` variable of the `Link` function so that we can run the same test on several links. To achieve this, we will replace the first line with the following:

```
with Browser("micclass:=Browser",
   "title:=Google").Page("title:=Google").Link("html
   tag:=A","innertext:="&DataTable("LinkText",
   dtLocalSheet))
```

Also, replace the last line with the following:

```
Browser("title:=.*"&DataTable("LinkText",
   dtLocalSheet)&".*").Back
```

3. We execute this code with a `DataTable` parameter called `LinkText` (refer to the *Creating a DataTable parameter* recipe in *Chapter 1, Data-driven Tests*) with three rows with the values `YouTube™`, `News`, and `Maps`. To set the Action to run on all rows, go to the **Test Flow** pane (from the menu navigate to **View | Test Flow**), and then right-click on `Action` and select **Action Call Properties...**, or navigate to **File | Settings**, select **Run** tab, and then select the **Run on all rows** option.

Note that in the last case, we concatenated an asterisk (*) before and after the `LinkText` parameter to match the `Browser` title, which adds `Google` before `News` and `Maps`. The inline description is treated by UFT as a regular expression by default.

How it works...

Instead of storing the TOs in OR, we use the `Browser`, `Page`, and `Link` objects and provide them either with a parameter string or a series of strings separated by commas, as shown in the previous section. These strings are used to build the description with which the objects are identified. First, the top level parent object (`Browser`), then `Page`, and finally, `Link` are identified. Take note of the syntax for the comma-separated property-value pairs in some of the descriptions.

Instead of hardcoded strings, such as `YouTube` for `innertext`, we concatenated a value taken from an external data source, namely `DataTable`, ran the test for several iterations (one link per `DataTable` row), and hence, tested that each link leads to the correct target. In our example, we check that our definition actually works by asking if it exists, and only then performing the `Highlight` and `Click` operations.

Using the Description object

The `Description` object is one of UFT's reserved objects, like the `Environment` and `Reporter` object. Basically, the `Description` object resembles a dictionary object with key-value pairs, which defines the properties and values by which the target TO or objects (see the *Using child objects* recipe), should be identified. Similar to the OR feature, the `Description` object also allows for regular expressions as property values. The following table shows regular expression samples of character property values:

User	To match character
\w	This represents a word character
\W	This represents a nonword character
\d	This represents a decimal digit
\D	This represents a nondecimal digit
\s	This represents a whitespace character
\S	This represents a nonwhitespace character

The `Description` object comes in handy in situations where the runtime object is dynamically built by the application, or when more complex criteria need to be applied to ascertain the identity of a TO among a collection of otherwise identical objects (for example, refer to the *Identifying elements based on anchors* recipe in *Chapter 2, Testing Web Pages*). Another application of the `Description` object is to get such a collection of objects and perform checkpoints to verify the values of specific properties.

Getting ready

Please ensure that the Internet Explorer application is open on Google.

How to do it...

We will identify the input query `WebEdit` object using a `Description` object. In `Action`, we will put the following code:

```
Set desc=Description.Create
desc("html tag").value="INPUT|input"
desc("html tag").RegularExpression = true
desc("name").value="q"

set oQuery=Browser("title:=Google").Page("title:=Google")
  .WebEdit(desc)

With oQuery
    If .exist(0) Then
        .highlight
    End If
End With
Set oQuery=nothing
Set desc=nothing
```

How it works...

We address the `WebEdit` parent objects using inline descriptions (refer to the *Using Descriptive Programming inline* recipe), and then target `WebEdit` using the `desc` `Description` object, which is used to identify the object using the property-value pairs. UFT returns a valid reference to the runtime object, exactly as it would if we used a TO stored in OR. Next, we check if the object reference exists and use the undocumented `highlight` method, which flashes a rectangle for a brief time around the target TO.

Using child objects

In the previous recipe, you have learned about using the `Description` object. This recipe will show you how to get a collection of runtime objects and perform checkpoints to verify the values of specific properties. In our example, we will describe how to retrieve images from a web page, and then perform a check operation using a `Checkpoint` object that we would store beforehand in OR.

How to do it...

Proceed with the following steps:

1. We will create a `Description` object and then define the appropriate property-value pairs for identification, as follows:

```
Dim oDesc, i, oImgCollection

Set oDesc=Description.Create
oDesc("html tag").value="IMG|img"
oDesc("html tag").RegularExpression = true
```

2. The following statement will retrieve a collection of images from the Google page:

```
set oImgCollection=Browser("title:=Google")
    .Page("title:=Google").ChildObjects(oDesc)
```

3. With this collection, we can now implement a loop that uses our `Checkpoint` object to validate the required properties:

```
For i = 0 To oImgCollection.count-1
    oImgCollection(i).Check(Checkpoint("Image"))
Next
```

How it works...

The `Description` object, `oDesc`, was created to cover objects having the HTML tag `img`. The page's `ChildObjects` method uses the `Description` object property's set definition to find a match with actual application (runtime) objects and returns a collection (array) of such objects. The items in this collection can be accessed using a zero-based index, as shown in the `For` loop (in the previous section), and different operations, such as `GetROProperty` and `WaitProperty`, can be applied to them. It is important to stress that these are runtime objects, and hence, trying to apply the methods `GetTOProperty`, `SetTOProperty`, and `GetTOProperties` is useless. This technique is useful when we need to perform a standard set of checks on different objects, as it optimizes our code syntax and allows for re-use of `Checkpoint` objects. Moreover, it accommodates future changes in the application, as the procedure operates on dynamically retrieved objects.

Using native properties for object identification

With UFT, it is very straightforward to access identification properties using `GetROProperty` and `CheckProperty`. However, this limits the scope of what can be checked, as TOs bring many properties that may be required. Fortunately, at least in web applications, we can also use native properties for object identification. In this recipe, we will demonstrate this feature using adapted examples from the previous recipes.

Getting ready

Please ensure that the Internet Explorer application is open on Google.

How to do it...

We will identify the input query `WebEdit` object using a `Description` object. In `Action`, we will put the following code:

```
Set desc=Description.Create
desc("attribute/nodeName").value="INPUT|input"
desc("attribute/nodeName").RegularExpression = true
desc("attribute/name").value="q"

set oQuery=Browser("title:=Google").Page("title:=Google")
  .WebEdit(desc)

With oQuery
    If .exist(0) Then
        .highlight
    End If
End With
Set oQuery=nothing
Set desc=nothing
```

How it works...

Basically, this code works exactly as detailed in the *Using the Description object* recipe. The difference is in the way we defined the properties in the `Description` object; while in the previous example we used identification properties, here we use native or runtime properties. The `attribute` (or prefix) variable indicates that it is a runtime property. Recall that the standard windows Test Objects lack runtime properties and object capabilities. The name of the property must be valid.

There's more...

The reader may ask, when would using native properties be useful? There are several cases in which it would be useful, as follows:

- First, there are cases where none of the TO properties provided by UFT yield robust, consistent object identification. In other cases, these properties are not reliable due to possible glitches. In such a case, the `Description` object identifier might be the last resort and the only possibility to achieve unique object identification.

- Second, it enables us to get the value of a native property without the need to use the `Object` property. For example:

```
ImgProtocol=Browser("App Perform").Page("Application
  Performance").Image("Precise").
  GetROProperty("attribute/protocol")
```

- There are cases where we would need to refer to the `UniqueID` native attribute, which is not even available through the UFT Spy. This property is similar to hWnd we know from Windows applications, and it can be useful when the default properties of an object change during the automation run session, making identification through parameterized properties very demanding. We would then identify the target object once, get `UniqueID`, and then use it across the runtime session. For example:

```
'Get the UniqueID for an identified Web element
ImgID=Browser("Browser").Page("Page").Image("Image").
  GetROProperty("attribute/UniqueID")

'Use the UniqueID with an inline description
Browser("Browser").Page("Page").Image("attribute/UniqueID:=
  "&ImgID).Click
```

See also

Refer to an article by Meir Bar-Tal at `http://www.advancedqtp.com/using-runtime-attributes-to-describe-qtp-web-objects/`.

Identifying an object based on its parent

In some cases, a TO may appear repeatedly on a window or page. A common example is images that are used as buttons in web applications. If a function is called to perform an action on such a TO, we may need to ensure that the correct object was passed. A powerful technique to achieve this is already outlined in the *Identifying elements based on anchors* recipe in *Chapter 2, Testing Web Pages*. In this recipe, we will see how to do it according to the object's parent (such as a `Frame` or `WebTable`, but can also be any `WebElement`), which is the container that holds our target TO.

How to do it...

Suppose that we have a reference to an OR TO and need to perform an operation or checkpoint using it and that we know the description of its container object. We can then write the following function that will indicate whether the target TO is the one we were looking for, based on its parent:

```
Function IsObjectByParent(ByVal obj, ByVal oDicProps)
    Dim bParent, oParent, prop

    Set oParent = obj.GetTOProperty("parent")
    bParent = true
    For each prop in oDicProps.keys
        If oDicProps(prop) <> oParent.GetTOProperty(prop) Then
            bParent = false
            Exit for
        End If
    Next

    IsObjectByParent=bParent
End Function
```

How it works...

Our function accepts two arguments, the target TO and a `Dictionary` object, with key-value pairs representing the properties and their respective expected values for the parent object. Using the `GetTOProperty` method, we dynamically retrieve the actual parent object of our referenced TO. Finally, we loop through the `Dictionary` keys and compare the expected value associated with each key to the corresponding TO property. We set the `bParent` flag variable as `true` (optimistic initialization), and in case any of its properties do not match the expected set, then it will fail and exit the `For` loop. The function returns `true` only if all parent properties match the expected set.

6
Event and Exception Handling

In this chapter, we will cover the following recipes:

- ▶ Catching errors inside a function or subroutine
- ▶ Creating and using a recovery scenario
- ▶ Using a global dictionary for recovery

Introduction

The topic of exception handling is extremely important, because the robustness of an automation suite affects its reliability. An automated test may fail due to unhandled and unexpected events, such as the appearance of a pop-up dialog or window, an application crash, or a runtime error (for example, due to poor quality code or an object description that is outdated). If you do not consider such possibilities while designing your scripts, then it will reflect on your ability to rely on the suite and accordingly reduce the return on investment/ effort of automation. For instance, a fragile, unstable automation suite may require attended run sessions, thus making one of the most prominent promises of automation (to free the manual tester for other tasks) void. This chapter will describe various techniques to handle events and exceptions.

Catching errors inside a function or subroutine

In this recipe, we will learn how to implement an error trap inside a function or subroutine.

Getting ready

From the **File** menu, navigate to **New | Function Library...** or use the *Alt + Shift + N* shortcut. Name the new function library `ErrHandling_Func.vbs`. You can use any other name, or reuse an existing function library. Do not forget to ensure that the library is attached to the test through **Resources** (**File | Settings | Resources**).

How to do it...

The technique is very simple. First, within your function, identify the line or lines of code that carry the potential of raising an exception (for example, an unhandled error). For instance, we write the following simple function to perform a division operation:

```
Function DblDivideXByY(x, y)
    'Return the result of the division as a Double
    DivideXByY=CDbl(x/y)
End function
```

The problem with the preceding code is that it assumes a priori that the parameters passed to the function are valid. However, there are at least two cases in which the function would fail to execute due to a runtime error:

- y=0
- x or y are not numeric

While it is possible to check for the possible sources of error (in the preceding code, by using the `isnumeric` function and checking if y is not equal to zero), it is in general an impractical approach. Unlike syntax errors, which can be found easily (by navigating to **Design | Check Syntax** from the UFT home page), runtime errors in VBScript pose a challenging threat to the robustness of our scripts. For example, suppose a function A calls another function B. If the interface of function B changes, say, an additional argument is added; then during runtime, the call would result in an error number of 450 (the wrong number of arguments or invalid property assignments). However, we will not be able to know this until function A is called.

Unlike other programming languages (such as C, C++, C#, and Java), VBScript is an untyped, late-bound language. Untyped means that variables are of a generic type called variant, and they assume a specific type only through assignment. By late-bound, we mean that the correctness of a statement is checked only during runtime. **Windows Script Host** (**WSH**) parses our script code line-by-line, and throws an error only at this stage. For our test script, this would be too late. However, we can use a feature of VBScript that allows us to disable the error checking mechanism during runtime, in order to handle the exceptions in a custom way that better suits our needs. This way, we set a trap to capture the error in a specific block of code, which we expect to be troublesome.

For those knowledgeable in other programming languages, this resembles the `try-catch` structure used to handle potential exceptions:

```
Function DblDivideXByY(x, y)
    const C_FUNC_NAME="DblDivideXByY"
    'Disable automatic runtime error-handling
    On error resume next
    'Return the result of the division as a Double
    DivideXByY=CDbl(x/y)
    'Check if an error was thrown
    If err.number <> 0 Then
        reporter.ReportEvent micFail, C_FUNC_NAME, err.description
        'TODO: Your handler
        'Example for general handling - Halt the run session
        ExitTest
    End If
    'Enable automatic runtime error-handling
    '(not a must since it's restored upon exiting the function)
    On error goto 0
End Function
```

We then call the `DblDivideXByY` function with the following lines of code:

```
'This is OK
print DblDivideXByY(5, 5)
'This will throw error number 11 (Divide by zero)
print DblDivideXByY(5, 0)
'This will throw error number 13 (Type mismatch)
print DblDivideXByY(5, "wrong")
```

How it works...

The custom method we implemented takes two arguments, x and y. The first is the dividend and the latter is the divisor. First, to obtain full control over the flow, we disable VBScript's native runtimeerror-handling mechanism with `On error resume next`. Then, we attempt to actually perform the division operation. If an error of any kind occurs, it will be caught by the clause `If err.number <> 0 Then`, and our customexception-handling code will be executed. In our example, we report a failure and stop the test when an error occurs, but the specific implementation one chooses depends on the requirements. For instance, the error may occur under controlled conditions (negative test), and hence, our implementation should be more complex to cover such situations. In any case, it is recommended to leave the function as simple as possible.

See also

Refer to the *Adding a new method to a class* recipe of *Chapter 4, Method Overriding*.

Creating and using a recovery scenario

UFT also enables us to define a specific behavior to handle a wide array of situations in advance. For example, instead of having to check our code for the existence of an unhandled pop-up dialog that may interfere with the normal flow of our test, we can use a recovery scenario to instruct UFT what to do if such is found. For example, we may tell UFT to close the dialog and try to rerun the step that failed due to the existence of the dialog. Another option, would be to tell UFT to exit the current Action or test iteration (in such cases, we must ensure that the test or Action begins in the proper context, that is, with the initial set of conditions). A simple case of a pop-up dialog is that of Notepad's warning when we try to close the application without having saved the document:

We can use a recovery scenario to handle the pop-up dialog, and this way, we will not have to refer to it in our code. The recovery scenario mechanism is a trap for the events we define as interfering with our test, which we call exceptions.

How to do it...

Proceed with the following steps:

1. From the home page of UFT, navigate to **Resources | Recovery Scenario Manager**. A dialog with the same title will open. Here, in the scenario frame, click on the **New** scenario button on the left-hand side of the toolbar:

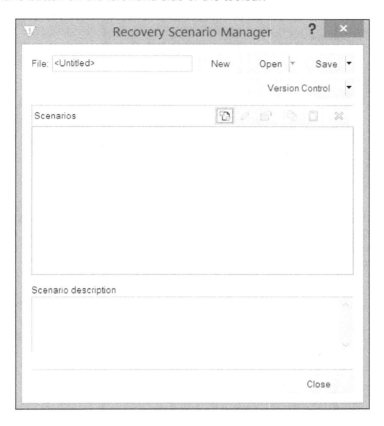

The **Recovery Scenario Wizard** window will then open up:

As it explicitly states, this wizard will guide you through the process of defining a recovery scenario for an unexpected event that needs to be handled, as it impedes your test from proceeding as planned. The wizard goes through four main stages.

2. First, we define the trigger event that interrupts the test run, which can be the appearance of an unexpected pop-up dialog, an object state, an unhandled test run error, or an application crash, as shown in the following screenshot:

3. Next, we specify the recovery operations required to continue, which can be a keyboard or a mouse operation, by closing an application process, calling a custom function, or even restarting windows:

4. For the sake of this example, we selected **Keyboard or mouse operation**, and pressed the *Enter* key. The operation is added to the list, as shown in the following screenshot:

Please note that leaving the **Add another recovery operation** checkbox marked allows for repetition of this step. If you need only a single recovery operation, then uncheck the checkbox:

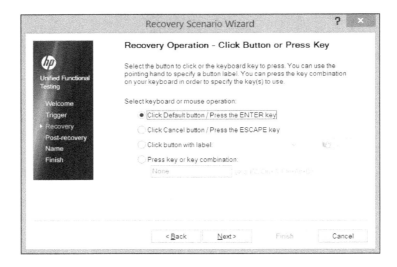

5. Next, is a post-recovery test run operation, which is related to UFT's built-in runtime mechanism and tells the tool what to do after the recovery operations are executed. It is imperative to analyze the requirement thoroughly for each particular case, because the options UFT offers would easily fail unless proper care is taken to ensure that test preconditions are kept. For example, there is no point in proceeding to the next test or Action iteration if the required application context is not guaranteed to show up at the start of the iteration. The following screenshot shows various post-recovery test run options:

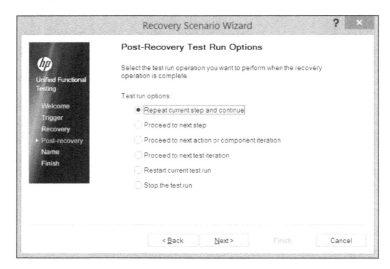

The **Post-Recovery Test Run Options** are:

- ❑ **Repeat current step and continue**: Actually, it is a retry mechanism, which raises the question of what would happen in the case of a recurring error. As no exit condition is provided, an infinite loop of error-recovery-retry-error is a real risk. The same procedure can be rewritten as a loop that repeats the error-causing statement (or block of code) until the error is eliminated. The code is as follows:

```
On Error Resume Next
'Statement that raises error
Do While Err.Number <> 0
'Statement that handles error
'Statement that raises error
Loop
```

- ❑ **Proceed to next step**: This test will attempt to execute after the step that gave rise to the error. The code equivalent of this option is the error-handling structure:

```
On Error Resume Next
'Statement that raises error
If Err.Number <> 0 Then
'Statement that handles error
End If
'The next statement
```

> Our test will still fail if the recovery operation does not succeed, or if it does, but for some reason the exact application context fit for the next step is not reached (for example, we handled a pop-up dialog by closing it, but the application opened another one or reopened the same pop-up as it reflected a real problem in the application, such as a script exception as is common on the Web).

- ❑ **Proceed to next action or component iteration**: This option allows you to run the next action or component iteration. As previously mentioned, we must ensure that the problem is specific to the case we have run, and that our recovery procedure, together with the iteration initialization, produces the initial conditions required for the next iteration to run.

- ❑ **Proceed to next test iteration**: This option allows you to run the next iteration and ensures that the recovery scenario (for example, closing the application or terminating its process) and the test iteration initialization always produce the conditions for the test to begin running from the first step (for example, opening the application, logging in, and so on).

- ❏ **Restart current test run**: This option allows you to restart the current test run. Some isolated glitches might cause a nonconsequential exception, which can be resolved by rerunning the test. However, if it is due to a real bug or some substantial infrastructure problem (for example, the server going down), then this will be to no avail.

- ❏ **Stop the test run**: This option allows you to stop the test run, but it enables analysis of the problem without having to review the effects of the exception on the next steps, hence allowing us to focus.

6. Next, we enter descriptive information about the scenario. Name the scenario and save it for future use as shown:

So far, we have used the step names exactly as they appear on screen:

Define the trigger event that interrupts the test run

Specify the recovery operations required to continue

Choose a post-recovery test run operation

7. Next, clicking on the **Next** button will lead to the following finish screen, in which we will check the option **Add scenario to current test**:

8. Now, click on **Finish**, which will return to the **Recovery Scenario Manager** dialog box:

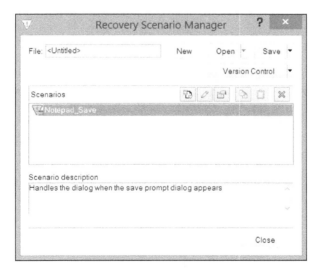

9. We will then save the scenario to a file by clicking on **Save**. The resulting QRS file will then be available to all relevant tests.

How it works...

The recovery scenario that we define will be loaded in memory and activated, unless we choose to deactivate it by unloading the attached ORS file or by using the following code:

```
Recovery.Enabled = False
```

We can set a recovery scenario to be activated on every step or on the occurrence of an error. A warning must be given here, as the first option may carry high costs regarding the performance of the test.

The test will run normally, while in parallel, the recovery mechanism will monitor to check whether the trigger event or events defined in our recovery scenarios actually occur. If they do, then the associated recovery procedure will be called into Action, and after its execution, the post-recovery operation, such as skipping to the next step, restarting the test run, or any of the other options detailed in the previous section, will be carried out.

Using a global dictionary for recovery

A powerful technique to implement the direct invocation of a recovery procedure makes an ingenious use of a global (public) `Dictionary` object. The method involves the use of command wrappers, function pointers, and callback functions. If you are not familiar with such object-oriented design patterns and concepts, then it is recommended that you first read *Chapter 7, Using Classes*, where some basic concepts are outlined.

The idea of using a dictionary to implement function pointers was first raised in an article published on `www.advancedqtp.com/` back in 2007. A `Dictionary` object is capable of storing data of any type, including objects and even other `Dictionary` objects, thus serving as a tree-like structure. It occurred to us that we might exploit this idea to store executable objects, which would run their code upon accessing their associated (hashed) keys. An executable object in VBScript can be built using the command wrapper design pattern, which encapsulates a process (function or subroutine) using a class. Another less elegant, yet effective way of building this feature is by means of storing references to functions using the `GetRef` method. So, in the event of an unexpected error, we may take advantage of such a data structure by means of mapping handling procedures to error numbers. The result is a hash table that stores the instructions of what to do in every case. It is also possible to store by the same method, procedures associated with unexpected events, which are not errors, such as the detection of a pop-up dialog. The advantages of this solution are obvious:

- It reduces the amount of code dedicated to reroute the test flow in case an error or any other unexpected event occurs.

- It provides a highly maintainable and clear way of handling exceptions and flow branching.

- It provides direct access to the event handler, instead of having to recur to ordinary function calls. All you have to do is retrieve the value associated with a key (the error or event), and the code is automatically executed.

The performance of such a mechanism outplays the ordinary recovery scenario procedures, as it is invoked **Just-in-Time** (**JIT**) without putting any burden on the machine's resources.

Getting ready

From the **File** menu, navigate to **New | Function Library...**, or use the *Alt + Shift + N* shortcut. Name the new function library `GlobalDic_Func.vbs`.

How to do it...

Proceed with the following steps:

1. In the function library, we will write the following code to implement the `EventHandlerManager` class, which will be loaded at the start of a run session:

```
Dim oEventHandlerManager

Function createEventHandlerManager()
    'Singleton
    If not lcase(typename(oEventHandlerManager)) =
      "eventHandlerManager" Then
        Set oEventHandlerManager=new EventHandlerManager
    End If
End Function

Function disposeEventHandlerManager()
    Set oEventHandlerManager=nothing
End Function

Class EventHandlerManager
    Public m_DicEvents

    Function Run(sEvent)
        Events.item(cstr(sEvent))(sEvent)
    End Function
```

```
Function mapHandlerToEvent(sEvent, sHandler)
    Events.Add sEvent, getHandler(sHandler)
End Function

Function getHandler(sHandler)
    Dim oHandler
    On error resume next
    Execute "set oHandler=new " & sHandler
    If err.number <> 0 Then
        Set oHandler=nothing
        reporter.ReportEvent micFail, typename(me) &
            ".getHandler", "Failed to load handler " &
            sHandler
    End If

    Set getHandler=oHandler
End Function

Property get Events()
    set Events=m_DicEvents
End Property

Property let Events(oHandlerManager)
    Set m_DicEvents=oHandlerManager
End Property

Sub class_initialize
    Events=createobject("Scripting.Dictionary")
End Sub
Sub class_terminate
    Events=nothing
End Sub
End Class
```

2. Now, add the following code (it can be in the same function library or a separate one) to implement a specific event handler:

```
Class MyHandler
    Public default Function Exec(sEvent)
        reporter.ReportEvent micDone, typename(me),
            "Handling event " & sEvent
        err.clear
        reporter.ReportEvent micDone, typename(me),
            "Handled event " & sEvent
    End Function
End Class
```

The event handler `MyHandler` reports the results and clears the error. For each specific error or event, we will implement such a class and map it using the `oEventHandlerManager` global object.

3. Now, we will see how to map our event handler to an event. As an example, we will use error number 9, which is division by zero:

```
createEventHandlerManager()

call oEventHandlerManager.mapHandlerToEvent("9",
    "MyHandler")

On error resume next

err.raise 9

oEventHandlerManager.Run(err.number)

disposeEventHandlerManager()
```

How it works...

We first create a global instance of `EventHandlerManager` in the global variable `oEventHandlerManager`. We then use the `mapHandlerToEvent` method to indicate that we wish to execute the code encapsulated in the `Exec` method of the `MyHandler` class. Then we raise an error, and finally, call the `Run` method of `EventHandlerManager` with the error number as an argument. Please notice that no `if-then-else` structure is used, so it actually can work as a kind of implicit try-catch mechanism. You are invited to try it with different errors and `EventHandler` implementations. For example, such a handler may halt the entire run session, or skip to the next Action iteration or test iteration. At last, we dispose off our `EventHandlerManager` class (this will be done only at the end of the test run).

The `EventHandlerManager` class is actually a wrapper to the dictionary. The member field `m_DicEvents` holds a reference to the dictionary, which stores key-value pairs (in this case, the keys being the error codes or other user-defined events), with the values being references to instances of the corresponding `EventHandler` classes.

As the `Exec` method of `EventHandler` (`MyHandler` in our example) is defined as the default, we do not need to write `Events.item(cstr(sEvent)).Exec(sEvent)` in the `Run` method of `EventHandlerManager`. It is sufficient to access the key by means of `Events.item(cstr(sEvent))(sEvent)`, and this triggers the default method. In this sense, it works like a function pointer, as mentioned earlier in this chapter.

It is, of course, important to note that in order to make this mechanism work infallibly, all `EventHandler` classes must follow the same basic structure as exemplified in the previous code with `MyHandler`. This means, any such class must contain a public default function named `Exec`.

7
Using Classes

In this chapter, we will cover the following recipes:

- ▶ Implementing a class
- ▶ Implementing a simple search class
- ▶ Implementing a generic Login class
- ▶ Implementing function pointers
- ▶ Implementing a generic Iterator

Introduction

This chapter describes how to use classes in VBScript, along with some very useful and illustrative implementation examples. Classes are a fundamental feature of object-oriented programming languages such as C++, C#, and Java. Classes enable us to encapsulate data fields with the methods and properties that process them, in contrast to global variables and functions scattered in function libraries. UFT already uses classes, such as with reserved objects (refer to *Chapter 8, Utility and Reserved Objects*), and Test Objects are also instances of classes. Although elementary object-oriented features such as inheritance and polymorphism are not supported by VBScript, using classes can be an excellent choice to make your code more structured, better organized, and more efficient and reusable.

Implementing a class

In this recipe, you will learn the following:

- ▶ The basic concepts and the syntax required by VBScript to implement a class
- ▶ The different components of a class and interoperation
- ▶ How to implement a type of generic constructor function for VBScript classes
- ▶ How to use a class during runtime

Getting ready

From the **File** menu, navigate to **New | Function Library...**, or use the *Alt + Shift + N* shortcut. Name the new function library cls.MyFirstClass.vbs and associate it with your test.

How to do it...

We will build our MyFirstClass class from the ground up. There are several steps one must follow to implement a class; they are follows:

1. Define the class as follows:

   ```
   Class MyFirstClass
   ```

2. Next, we define the class fields. Fields are like regular variables, but encapsulated within the namespace defined by the class. The fields can be private or public. A private field can be accessed only by class members. A public field can be accessed from any block of code. The code is as follows:

   ```
   Class MyFirstClass
      Private m_sMyPrivateString
      Private m_oMyPrivateObject
      Public m_iMyPublicInteger
   End Class
   ```

 It is a matter of convention to use the prefix m_ for class member fields; and str for string, int for integer, obj for Object, flt for Float, bln for Boolean, chr for Character, lng for Long, and dbl for Double, to distinguish between fields of different data types. For examples of other prefixes to represent additional data types, please refer to sites such as https://en.wikipedia.org/wiki/Hungarian_notation.

Hence, the private fields' `m_sMyPrivateString` and `m_oMyPrivateObject` will be accessible only from within the class methods, properties, and subroutines. The public field `m_iMyPublicInteger` will be accessible from any part of the code that will have a reference to an instance of the `MyFirstClass` class; and it can also allow partial or full access to private fields, by implementing public properties.

> By default, within a script file, VBScript treats as public identifiers such as function and subroutines and any constant or variable defined with `Const` and `Dim` respectively, even if not explicitly defined. When associating function libraries to UFT, one can limit access to specific globally defined identifiers, by preceding them with the keyword `Private`.
>
> The same applies to members of a class, function, sub, and property. Class fields must be preceded either by `Public` or `Private`; the public scope is not assumed by VBScript, and failing to precede a field identifier with its access scope will result in a syntax error. Remember that, by default, VBScript creates a new variable if the explicit option is used at the script level to force explicit declaration of all variables in that script level.

3. Next, we define the class properties. A property is a code structure used to selectively provide access to a class' private member fields. Hence, a property is often referred to as a getter (to allow for data retrieval) or setter (to allow for data change).

    A property is a special case in VBScript; it is the only code structure that allows for a duplicate identifier. That is, one can have a `Property Get` and a `Property Let` procedure (or `Property Set`, to be used when the member field actually is meant to store a reference to an instance of another class) with the same identifier. Note that `Property Let` and `Property Set` accept a mandatory argument. For example:

```
Class MyFirstClass
   Private m_sMyPrivateString
   Private m_oMyPrivateObject
   Public m_iMyPublicInteger

   Property Get MyPrivateString()
     MyPrivateString = m_sMyPrivateString
   End Property

   Property Let MyPrivateString(ByVal str)
     m_sMyPrivateString = str
   End Property

   Property Get MyPrivateObject()
     Set MyPrivateObject = m_oMyPrivateObject
   End Property
```

```
       Private Property Set MyPrivateObject(ByRef obj)
         Set m_oMyPrivateObject = obj
       End Property
    End Class
```

The public field m_iMyPublicInteger can be accessed from any code block, so defining a getter and setter (as properties are often referred to) for such a field is optional. However, it is a good practice to define fields as private and explicitly provide access through public properties. For fields that are for exclusive use of the class members, one can define the properties as private. In such a case, usually, the setter (Property Let or Property Set) would be defined as private, while the getter (Property Get) would be defined as public. This way, one can prevent other code components from making changes to the internal fields of the class to ensure data integrity and validity.

4. Define the class methods and subroutines. A method is a function, which is a member of a class. Like fields and properties, methods (as well as subroutines) can be Private or Public. For example:

```
Class MyFirstClass
  '... Continued
  Private Function MyPrivateFunction(ByVal str)
    MsgBox TypeName(me) & " - Private Func: " & str
    MyPrivateFunction = 0
  End Function

  Function MyPublicFunction(ByVal str)
    MsgBox TypeName(me) & " - Public Func: " & str
    MyPublicFunction = 0
  End Function

  Sub MyPublicSub(ByVal str)
    MsgBox TypeName(me) & " - Public Sub: " & str
  End Sub
End Class
```

Keep in mind that subroutines do not return a value. Functions by design should not return a value, but they can be implemented as a subroutine. A better way is to, in any case, have a function return a value that tells the caller if it executed properly or not (usually zero (0) for no errors and one (1) for any fault). Recall that a function that is not explicitly assigned a value function and is not explicitly assigned a value, will return empty, which may cause problems if the caller attempts to evaluate the returned value.

5. Now, we define how to initialize the class when a VBScript object is instantiated:

```
Set obj = New MyFirstClass
```

The `Initialize` event takes place at the time the object is created. It is possible to add code that we wish to execute every time an object is created. So, now define the standard private subroutine `Class_Initialize`, sometimes referred to (albeit only by analogy) as the constructor of the class. If implemented, the code will automatically be executed during the `Initialize` event. For example, if we add the following code to our class:

```
Private Sub Class_Initialize
  MsgBox TypeName(me) & " started"
End Sub
```

Now, every time the `Set obj = New MyFirstClass` statement is executed, the following message will be displayed:

6. Define how to finalize the class. We finalize a class when a VBScript object is disposed of (as follows), or when the script exits the current scope (such as when a local object is disposed when a function returns control to the caller), or a global object is disposed (when UFT ends its run session):

```
Set obj = Nothing
```

The `Finalize` event takes place at the time when the object is removed from memory. It is possible to add code that we wish to execute, every time an object is disposed of. If so, then define the standard private subroutine `Class_Terminate`, sometimes referred to (albeit only by analogy) as the destructor of the class. If implemented, the code will automatically be executed during the `Finalize` event. For example, if we add the following code to our class:

```
Private Sub Class_Terminate
  MsgBox TypeName(me) & " ended"
End Sub
```

Now, every time the `Set obj = Nothing` statement is executed, the following message will be displayed:

7. Invoking (calling) a class method or property is done as follows:

```
'Declare variables
Dim obj, var

'Calling MyPublicFunction
obj.MyPublicFunction("Hello")

'Retrieving the value of m_sMyPrivateString
var = obj.MyPrivateString

'Setting the value of m_sMyPrivateString
obj.MyPrivateString = "My String"
```

Note that the usage of the public members is done by using the syntax `obj.<method or property name>`, where `obj` is the variable holding the reference to the object of class. The dot operator (`.`) after the variable identifier provides access to the public members of the class. Private members can be called only by other members of the class, and this is done like any other regular function call.

8. VBScript supports classes with a default behavior. To utilize this feature, we need to define a single default method or property that will be invoked every time an object of the class is referred to, without specifying which method or property to call. For example, if we define the public method `MyPublicFunction` as default:

```
Public Default Function MyPublicFunction(ByVal str)
  MsgBox TypeName(me) & " - Public Func: " & str
  MyPublicFunction = 0
End Function
```

Now, the following statements would invoke the `MyPublicFunction` method implicitly:

```
Set obj = New MyFirstClass

obj("Hello")
```

This is exactly the same as if we called the `MyPublicFunction` method explicitly:

```
Set obj = New MyFirstClass

obj.MyPublicFunction("Hello")
```

 Contrary to the usual standard for such functions, a default method or property must be explicitly defined as `public`.

9. Now, we will see how to add a constructor-like function. When using classes stored in function libraries, UFT (know as QTP in previous versions), cannot create an object using the `New` operator inside a test Action.

    In general, the reason is linked to the fact that UFT uses a wrapper on top of WSH, which actually executes the VBScript (VBS 5.6) code. Therefore, in order to create instances of such a custom class, we need to use a kind of constructor function that will perform the `New` operation from the proper memory namespace. Add the following generic constructor to your function library:

```
Function Constructor(ByVal sClass)
  Dim obj

  On Error Resume Next

  'Get instance of sClass
  Execute "Set obj = New [" & sClass & "]"
  If Err.Number <> 0 Then
    Set obj = Nothing
    Reporter.ReportEvent micFail, "Constructor", "Failed
      to create an instance of class '" & sClass & "'."
  End If

  Set Constructor = obj
End Function
```

We will then instantiate the object from the UFT Action, as follows:

```
Set obj = Constructor("MyFirstClass")
```

Consequently, use the object reference in the same fashion as seen in the previous line of code:

```
obj.MyPublicFunction("Hello")
```

How it works...

As mentioned earlier, using the internal public fields, methods, subroutines, and properties is done using a variable followed by the dot operator and the relevant identifier (for example, the function name).

As to the constructor, it accepts a string with the name of a class as an argument, and attempts to create an instance of the given class. By using the `Execute` command (which performs any string containing valid VBScript syntax), it tries to set the variable `obj` with a new reference to an instance of `sClass`. Hence, we can handle any custom class with this function. If the class cannot be instantiated (for instance, because the string passed to the function is faulty, the function library is not associated to the test, or there is a syntax error in the function library), then an error would arise, which is gracefully handled by using the error-handling mechanism (as described in *Chapter 6, Event and Exception Handling*), leading to the function returning nothing. Otherwise, the function will return a valid reference to the newly created object.

See also

The following articles at `www.advancedqtp.com` are part of a wider collection, which also discuss classes and code design in depth:

▶ An article by Yaron Assa at `http://www.advancedqtp.com/introduction-to-classes`

▶ An article by Yaron Assa at `http://www.advancedqtp.com/introduction-to-code-design`

▶ An article by Yaron Assa at `http://www.advancedqtp.com/introduction-to-design-patterns`

Implementing a simple search class

In this recipe, we will see how to create a class that can be used to execute a search on Google.

Getting ready

From the **File** menu, navigate to **New | Test**, and name the new test `SimpleSearch`. Then, create a new function library by navigating to **New | Function Library**, or use the *Alt + Shift + N* shortcut. Name the new function library `cls.Google.vbs` and associate it with your test.

How to do it...

Proceed with the following steps:

1. Define an environment variable as `OPEN_URL`.

2. Insert the following code in the new library:

```
Class GoogleSearch
  Public Function DoSearch(ByVal sQuery)
    With me.Page_
      .WebEdit("name:=q").Set sQuery
      .WebButton("html id:=gbqfba").Click
    End With
    me.Browser_.Sync

    If me.Results.WaitProperty("visible", 1, 10000) Then
      DoSearch = GetNumResults()
    Else
      DoSearch = 0
      Reporter.ReportEvent micFail, TypeName(Me), _
        "Search did not retrieve results until timeout"
    End If
  End Function
```

```
Public Function GetNumResults()
  Dim tmpStr

  tmpStr = me.Results.GetROProperty("innertext")
  tmpStr = Split(tmpStr, " ")
  GetNumResults = CLng(tmpStr(1)) 'Assumes the number
    is always in the second entry
End Function

Public Property Get Browser_()
  Set Browser_ = Browser(me.Title)
End Property
Public Property Get Page_()
  Set Page_ = me.Browser_.Page(me.Title)
End Property
Public Property Get Results()
  Set Results = me.Page_.WebElement(me.ResultsId)
End Property
Public Property Get ResultsId()
  ResultsId = "html id:=resultStats"
End Property
Public Property Get Title()
  Title = "title:=.*Google.*"
End Property

Private Sub Class_Initialize
  If Not me.Browser_.Exist(0) Then
    SystemUtil.Run "iexplore.exe",
      Environment("OPEN_URL")
    Reporter.Filter = rfEnableErrorsOnly
    While Not Browser_.Exist(0)
      Wait 0, 50
    Wend
    Reporter.Filter = rfEnableAll
    Reporter.ReportEvent micDone, TypeName(Me),
      "Opened browser"
  Else
    Reporter.ReportEvent micDone, TypeName(Me),
      "Browser was already open"
  End If
End Sub
```

```
      Private Sub Class_Terminate
        If me.Browser_.Exist(0) Then
          me.Browser_.Close
          Reporter.Filter = rfEnableErrorsOnly
          While me.Browser_.Exist(0)
            wait 0, 50
          Wend
          Reporter.Filter = rfEnableAll
          Reporter.ReportEvent micDone, TypeName(Me), _
            "Closed browser"
        End If
      End Sub
    End Class
```

3. In Action, write the following code:

```
Dim oGoogleSearch
Dim oListResults
Dim oDicSearches
Dim iNumResults
Dim sMaxResults
Dim iMaxResults

'--- Create these objects only in the first iteration
If Not LCase(TypeName(oListResults)) = "arraylist" Then
  Set oListResults = _
    CreateObject("System.Collections.ArrayList")
End If

If Not LCase(TypeName(oDicSearches)) = "Dictionary" Then
  Set oDicSearches = CreateObject("Scripting.Dictionary")
End If

'--- Get a fresh instance of GoogleSearch
Set oGoogleSearch = GetGoogleSearch()

'--- Get search term from the DataTable for each action
  iteration
sToSearch = DataTable("Query", dtLocalSheet)
iNumResults = oGoogleSearch.DoSearch(sToSearch)

'--- Store the results of the current iteration
'--- Store the number of results
```

```
oListResults.Add iNumResults
'--- Store the search term attached to the number of
  results as key (if not exists)
If Not oDicSearches.Exists(iNumResults) Then
  oDicSearches.Add iNumResults, sToSearch
End If
'Last iteration (assuming we always run on all rows), so
  perform the comparison between the different searches

If CInt(Environment("ActionIteration")) =
  DataTable.LocalSheet.GetRowCount Then
  'Sort the results ascending
  oListResults.Sort
  'Get the last item which is the largest
  iMaxResults = oListResults.item(oListResults.Count-1)
  'Print to the Output pane for debugging
  Print iMaxResults
  'Get the search text which got the most results
  sMaxResults = oDicSearches(iMaxResults)
  'Report result
  Reporter.ReportEvent micDone, "Max search", sMaxResults
    & " got " & iMaxResults
  'Dispose of the objects used
  Set oListResults = Nothing
  Set oDicSearches = Nothing
  Set oGoogleSearch = Nothing
End If
```

4. In the local datasheet, create a parameter named Query and enter several values to be used in the test as search terms.

5. Next, from the UFT home page navigate to **View | Test Flow**, and then right-click with the mouse on the Action component in the graphic display, then select **Action Call Properties** and set the Action to run on all rows.

How it works...

The Action takes care to preserve the data collected through the iterations in the array list oListResults and the dictionary oDicSearches. It checks if it reaches the last iteration after each search is done. Upon reaching the last iteration, it analyzes the data to decide which term yielded the most results. A more detailed description of the workings of the code can be seen as follows.

First, we create an instance of the `GoogleSearch` class, and the `Class_Initialize` subroutine automatically checks if the browser is not already open. If not open, `Class_Initialize` opens it with the `SystemUtil.Run` command and waits until it is open at the web address defined in `Environment("OPEN_URL")`.

The `Title` property always returns the value of the **Descriptive Programming (DP)** value required to identify the Google browser and page.

The `Browser_`, `Page_`, and `Results` properties always return a reference to the Google browser, page, and `WebElement` respectively, which hold the text with the search results.

After the browser is open, we retrieve the search term from the local DataTable parameter `Query` and call the `GoogleSearch DoSearch` method with the search term string as parameter. The `DoSearch` method returns a value with the number of results, which are given by the internal method `GetNumResults`.

In the Action, we store the number itself and add to the dictionary, an entry with this number as the key and the search term as the value.

When the last iteration is reached, an analysis of the results is automatically done by invoking the `Sort` method of `oListResults ArrayList`, getting the last item (the greatest), and then retrieving the search term associated with this number from the dictionary; it reports the result.

At last, we dispose off all the objects used, and then the `Class_Terminate` subroutine automatically checks if the browser is open. If open, then the `Class_Terminate` subroutine closes the browser.

Implementing a generic Login class

In this recipe, we will see how to implement a generic `Login` class. The class captures both, the GUI structure and the processes that are common to all applications with regard to their user access module. It is agnostic to the particular object classes, their technologies, and other identification properties. The class shown here implements the command wrapper design pattern, as it encapsulates a process (`Login`) with the main default method (`Run`).

Getting ready

You can use the same function library `cls.Google.vbs` as in the previous recipe *Implementing a simple search class*, or create a new one (for instance, `cls.Login.vbs`) and associate it with your test.

1. In the function library, we will write the following code to define the class `Login`:

```
Class Login
    Private m_wndContainer  'Such as a Browser, Window,
      SwfWindow
    Private m_wndLoginForm  'Such as a Page, Dialog,
      SwfWindow
    Private m_txtUsername  'Such as a WebEdit, WinEdit,
      SwfEdit
    Private m_txtIdField  'Such as a WebEdit, WinEdit,
      SwfEdit
    Private m_txtPassword  'Such as a WebEdit, WinEdit,
      SwfEdit
    Private m_chkRemember  'Such as a WebCheckbox,
      WinCheckbox, SwfCheckbox
    Private m_btnLogin  'Such as a WebEdit, WinEdit,
      SwfEdit
End Class
```

These fields define the test objects, which are required for any `Login` class, and the following fields are used to keep runtime data for the report:

```
Public  Status  'As Integer
Public  Info  'As String
```

The `Run` function is defined as a `Default` method that accepts a `Dictionary` as argument. This way, we can pass a set of named arguments, some of which are optional, such as `timeout`.

```
Public Default Function Run(ByVal ArgsDic)
    'Check if the timeout parameter was passed, if not
      assign it 10 seconds
    If Not ArgsDic.Exists("timeout") Then ArgsDic.Add
      "timeout", 10
    'Check if the client window exists
    If Not me.Container.Exist(ArgsDic("timeout")) Then
      me.Status  = micFail
      me.Info  = "Failed to detect login
        browser/dialog/window."
      Exit Function
    End If
    'Set the Username
    me.Username.Set ArgsDic("Username")
    'If the login form has an additional mandatory field
```

```
      If me.IdField.Exist(ArgsDic("timeout")) And
        ArgsDic.Exists("IdField") Then
          me.IdField.Set ArgsDic("IdField")
      End If
      'Set the password
      me.Password.SetSecure ArgsDic("Password")
      'It is a common practice that Login forms have a
        checkbox to keep the user logged-in if set ON
      If me.Remember.Exist(ArgsDic("timeout")) And
        ArgsDic.Exists("Remember") Then
          me.Remember.Set ArgsDic("Remember")
      End If
      me.LoginButton.Click
    End Function
```

The `Run` method actually performs the login procedure, setting the username and password, as well as checking or unchecking the **Remember Me** or **Keep me Logged In** checkbox according to the argument passed with the `ArgsDic` dictionary.

The `Initialize` method accepts `Dictionary` just like the `Run` method. However, in this case, we pass the actual TOs with which we wish to perform the login procedure. This way, we can actually utilize the class for any `Login` form, whatever the technology used to develop it. We can say that the class is *technology agnostic*. The parent client dialog/browser/window of the objects is retrieved using the `GetTOProperty("parent")` statement:

```
Function Initialize(ByVal ArgsDic)
    Set m_txtUsername  = ArgsDic("Username")
    Set m_txtIdField   = ArgsDic("IdField")
    Set m_txtPassword  = ArgsDic("Password")
    Set m_btnLogin     = ArgsDic("LoginButton")
    Set m_chkRemember  = ArgsDic("Remember")
    'Get Parents
    Set m_wndLoginForm =
      me.Username.GetTOProperty("parent")
    Set m_wndContainer =
      me.LoginForm.GetTOProperty("parent")
  End Function
```

In addition, here you can see the following properties used in the class for better readability:

```
Property Get Container()
    Set Container = m_wndContainer
  End Property
  Property Get LoginForm()
```

```
      Set LoginForm = m_wndLoginForm
    End Property
    Property Get Username()
      Set Username = m_txtUsername
    End Property
    Property Get IdField()
      Set IdField = m_txtIdField
    End Property
    Property Get Password()
      Set Password = m_txtPassword
    End Property
    Property Get Remember()
      Set Remember = m_chkRemember
    End Property
    Property Get LoginButton()
      Set LoginButton = m_btnLogin
    End Property

    Private Sub Class_Initialize()
      'TODO: Additional initialization code here
    End Sub
    Private Sub Class_Terminate()
      'TODO: Additional finalization code here
    End Sub
```

We will also add a custom function to override the `WinEdit` and `WinEditor` Type methods:

```
Function WinEditSet(ByRef obj, ByVal str)
  obj.Type str
End Function
```

This way, no matter which technology the textbox belongs to, the `Set` method will work seamlessly.

2. To actually test the `Login` class, write the following code in the Test Action (this time we assume that the `Login` form was already opened by another procedure):

```
Dim ArgsDic, oLogin

'Register the set method for the WinEdit and WinEditor
RegisterUserFunc "WinEdit", "WinEditSet", "Set"
RegisterUserFunc "WinEditor", "WinEditSet", "Set"
```

```
'Create a Dictionary object
Set ArgsDic = CreateObject("Scripting.Dictionary")
'Create a Login object
Set oLogin = New Login

'Add the test objects to the Dictionary
With ArgsDic
    .Add "Username",
      Browser("Gmail").Page("Gmail").WebEdit("txtUsername")
    .Add "Password",
      Browser("Gmail").Page("Gmail").WebEdit("txtPassword")
    .Add "Remember",
      Browser("Gmail").Page("Gmail")
      .WebCheckbox("chkRemember")
    .Add "LoginButton",
      Browser("Gmail").Page("Gmail").WebButton("btnLogin")
End With

'Initialize the Login class
oLogin.Initialize(ArgsDic)

'Initialize the dictionary to pass the arguments to the
  login
ArgsDic.RemoveAll
With ArgsDic
    .Add "Username", "myuser"
    .Add "Password", "myencriptedpassword"
    .Add "Remember", "OFF"
End With

'Login
oLogin.Run(ArgsDic) 'or: oLogin(ArgsDic)

'Report result
Reporter.ReportEvent oLogin.Status, "Login", "Ended with "
  & GetStatusText(oLogin.Status) & "." & vbNewLine &
  oStatus.Info

'Dispose of the objects
Set oLogin = Nothing
Set ArgsDic = Nothing
```

How it works...

Here, we will not delve into the parts of the code already explained in the *Implementing a simple search class* recipe. Let's see what we did in this recipe:

 ▶ We registered the custom function `WinEditSet` to the `WinEdit` and `WinEditor` TO classes using `RegisterUserFunc`. As discussed previously, this will make every call to the method set to be rerouted to our custom function, resulting in applying the correct method to the Standard Windows text fields.

 ▶ Next, we created the objects we need, a `Dictionary` object and a `Login` object.

 ▶ Then, we added the required test objects to `Dictionary`, and then invoked its `Initialize` method, passing the `Dictionary` as the argument.

 ▶ We cleared `Dictionary` and then added to it the values needed for actually executing the login (`Username`, `Password`, and the whether to remember the user or keep logged in checkboxes usually used in `Login` forms).

 ▶ We called the `Run` method for the `Login` class with the newly populated `Dictionary`.

 ▶ Later, we reported the result by taking the `Status` and `Info` public fields from the `oLogin` object.

 ▶ At the end of the script, we unregistered the custom function from all classes in the environment (`StdWin` in this case).

Implementing function pointers

What is a function pointer? A function pointer is a variable that stores the memory address of a block of code that is programmed to fulfill a specific function. Function pointers are useful to avoid complex switch case structures. Instead, they support direct access in runtime to previously loaded functions or class methods. This enables the construction of callback functions. A callback is, in essence, an executable code that is passed as an argument to a function. This enables more generic coding, by having lower-level modules calling higher-level functions or subroutines.

This recipe will describe how to implement function pointers in VBScript, a scripting language that does not natively support the usage of pointers.

Getting ready

Create a new function library (for instance, `cls.FunctionPointers.vbs`) and associate it with your test.

How to do it...

1. Write the following code in the function library:

```
Class WebEditSet
    Public Default Function Run(ByRef obj, ByVal sText)
        On Error Resume Next
        Run = 1 'micFail (pessimistic initialization)
        Select Case True
            Case    obj.Exist(0) And _
                    obj.GetROProperty("visible") And _
                    obj.GetROProperty("enabled")
                    'Perform the set operation
                    obj.Set(sText)
            Case Else
                Reporter.ReportEvent micWarning, _
                    TypeName(me), "Object not available."
                Exit Function
        End Select

        If Err.Number = 0 Then
            Run = 0 'micPass
        End If
    End Function
End Class
```

2. Write the following code in `Action`:

```
Dim pFunctiontion
Set pFunctiontion = New WebEditSet
Reporter.ReportEvent
    pFunctiontion(Browser("Google").Page("Google")
    .WebEdit("q"), "UFT"), "Set the Google Search WebEdit",
    "Done"
```

How it works...

The `WebEditSet` class actually implements the command wrapper design pattern (refer also to the *Implementing a generic Login class* recipe). This recipe also demonstrates an alternative way of overriding any native UFT TO method without recurring to the `RegisterUserFunc` method.

First, we create an instance of the `WebEditSet` class and set the reference to our `pFunctiontion` variable. Note that the `Run` method of `WebEditSet` is declared as a default function, so we can invoke its execution by merely referring to the object reference, as is done with the statement `pFunctiontion` in the last line of code in the *How to do it...* section. This way, `pFunctiontion` actually functions as if it were a function pointer. Let us take a close look at the following line of code, beginning with `Reporter.ReportEvent`:

```
Reporter.ReportEvent
    pFunc(Browser("Google").Page("Google").WebEdit("q"), "UFT"),
    "Set the Google Search WebEdit", "Done"
```

We call the `ReportEvent` method of `Reporter`, and as its first parameter, instead of a status constant such as `micPass` or `micFail`, we pass `pFunctiontion` and the arguments accepted by the `Run` method (the target TO and its parameter, a string). This way of using the function pointer actually implements a kind of callback. The value returned by the `Run` method of `WebEditSet` will determine whether UFT will report a success or failure in regard to the `Set` operation. It will return through the call invoked by accessing the function pointer.

See also

The following articles are part of a wider collection at `www.advancedqtp.com`, which also discusses function pointers in depth:

- ▶ An article by Meir Bar-Tal at `http://www.advancedqtp.com/ function-pointers-in-vb-script-revised`
- ▶ An article by Meir Bar-Tal at `http://www.advancedqtp.com/using-to-custom-property-as-function-pointer`

Implementing a generic Iterator

This recipe will describe how to implement a mechanism that is able to execute any operation for objects of any class repeatedly, until a condition is met or until the whole queue of objects is processed. The condition can be any expression that results in a Boolean value.

Getting ready

Create a new function library (for instance, `cls.Iterator.vbs`), and associate it with your test. In this recipe, we shall use the code from the previous recipe, *Implementing function pointers*.

How to do it...

Proceed with the following steps:

1. In the function library, write the following code:

```
Class Iterator
    Public Default Function Run(ByRef oCollection, _
            ByRef ptrFunction, _
            ByVal dicArgs, _
            ByVal sExitCondition)

        Dim count, items, ix, str, dicResults

        'Create a Dictionary to store the results for each
          iteration
        Set dicResults =
          CreateObject("Scripting.Dictionary")

        'Get the collection count
        count = oCollection.Count

        'Get the object collection items
        items = oCollection.Items

        'Get the object collection keys
        keys = oCollection.Keys

        ix = 0
        Do While ix < count
            'Check if the exit condition holds true
            If Eval(sExitCondition) Then
                dicResults(keys(ix)) = "Iteration " & ix+1
                  & " not performed on object " & keys(ix)
                    & "." & _
                        vbNewLine & "Exit condition '" &
                          sExitCondition & "' holds true.
                          Exiting iterator."
                Exit Do
            End If

            'This statement performs the process/operation
              on the current item
            dicResults(keys(ix)) = ptrFunction(items(ix),
              dicArgs(keys(ix)))
```

```
                    'Increment the counter
                    ix = ix + 1
            Loop

            'Return Dictionary with the results
            Set Run = dicResults
        End Function
    End Class
```

2. In `Action`, write the following code:

```
Dim dicObjects
Dim dicArgs
Dim pFunc
Dim iter
Dim sExitCond
Dim key, keys

'Set the instances of the required objects
Set iter = New Iterator
Set dicObjects = CreateObject("Scripting.Dictionary")
Set dicArgs = CreateObject("Scripting.Dictionary")
Set pFunc = New WebEditSet

'Assign the string with the end condition
sExitCond = "Err.Number <> 0"

'Add the Test Objects to Dictionary dicObjects
dicObjects.Add "MyFirstObject", _
    Browser("MyBrowser").Page("MyPage").WebEdit("Edit1")
dicObjects.Add "MySecondObject", _
    Browser("MyBrowser").Page("MyPage").WebEdit("Edit2")
dicObjects.Add "MyThirdObject", _
    Browser("MyBrowser").Page("MyPage").WebEdit("Edit3")

'Add the strings to be passed as arguments to Dictionary
  dicArgs
dicArgs.Add "MyFirstObject", "One"
dicArgs.Add "MySecondObject", "Two"
dicArgs.Add "MyThirdObject", "Three"
```

```
'Call the iterator default function (as a function pointer)
   with its arguments
Call iter(dicObjects, pFunc, dicArgs, sExitCond)

'Dispose of the objects
Set dicArgs = Nothing
Set dicObjects = Nothing
Set pFunc = Nothing
Set iter = Nothing
```

 In our example, we do not store the value returned by the Run method (a dictionary) of Iterator. However, this can be done by assigning it to a variable using Set.

How it works...

The Iterator class has a default Run method, similar to what we have seen in the previous recipes. This method implements a loop that performs the operation defined by pFunctiontion for all objects in the collection defined by dicObjects, or until the exit condition defined by sExitCondition is reached. For each function call, it passes the corresponding argument, as defined in dicArguments (To handle functions accepting multiple arguments, one may simply send an array of values, instead of a single one as done here, and handle them within the target Run method of our custom command wrapper.).

The command wrapper WebEditSet (refer to the previous recipe) accepts as arguments a reference to the Test Object for which we wish to invoke the Set method and a string to be entered to the WebEdit object. So, what is actually going on here? The Iterator class passes to the Run method of WebEditSet the arguments it needs to perform the Set operation. The Iterator class is agnostic of the internals of the called method, except that it expects a return value. In this sense, it is absolutely generic.

8
Utility and Reserved Objects

In this chapter, we will cover the following recipes:

- ▸ Using global variables (Environment)
- ▸ Customizing mouse operations (DeviceReplay)
- ▸ Managing processes (SystemUtil)
- ▸ Measuring time (MercuryTimers)
- ▸ Resolving file locations (PathFinder)
- ▸ Loading shared object repositories (RepositoriesCollection)
- ▸ Loading and creating XML documents (XMLUtil)
- ▸ Drawing a rectangle on the screen with Win32 API methods (Extern)
- ▸ Verifying binary file contents (FileCompare)
- ▸ Implementing a custom reserved object
- ▸ Using remote objects
- ▸ Utility statements

Introduction

This chapter describes how to use the utility and reserved objects included in UFT replace with out-of-the-box. These objects are loaded automatically on launching UFT, so that their methods and properties are accessible immediately. There is a wide array of reserved objects, which offer services to utilize mouse and keyboard, system processes, files of different types, object repositories, time, APIs, and so on.

In addition, UFT supports custom-reserved objects, thus enabling the development of extensions to the basic out-of-the-box functionality. We will also give a step-by-step account of how this can be accomplished.

Using global variables (Environment)

The `Environment` object can be best described as a kind of **Dictionary** that holds pairs of keys and values. Unlike the native Dictionary, it has extended capacities such as the following:

> ▸ UFT features that contain built-in variables, which can return useful values during runtime, such as `ActionName`, `ActionIteration`, `TestName`, `TestIteration`, `TestDir`, and `OS`

> ▸ Defining test internal variables (that is, persistent) or external variables (see the following point)

> ▸ Loading a set of variables from an external XML file, preset, or dynamically used during runtime

> ▸ **Automation Object Model** (**AOM**) support, which enables the addition of internal variables dynamically before launching a test's run session

> ▸ The scope of the object is global and is loaded automatically when UFT opens, as is true for all reserved objects

Getting ready

From the **File** menu, navigate to **New** | **Test**, or use the *Ctrl + N* shortcut.

How to do it...

Proceed with the following steps:

1. For built-in variables:

    1. Navigate to **File | Settings**. The **Test Settings** dialog will open, as shown in the following screenshot. The **Environment** item (tab) is circled in red:

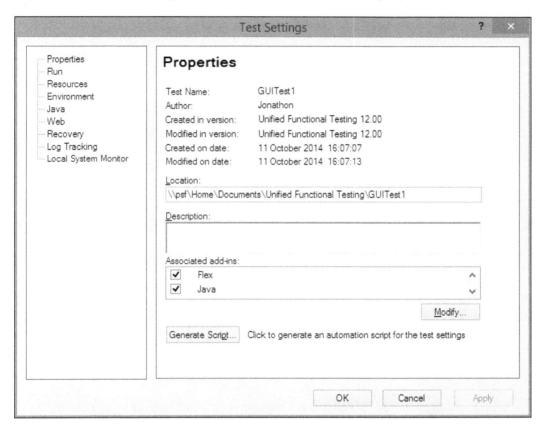

2. Select **Environment**, as shown in the previous screenshot, and the dialog will display the built-in variables list. Scroll to explore the variables. Take note that the list here is a field labelled **Current value**, which will show the variable's value only if it is not a runtime determined value. Examples for the latter are `ActionIteration` and `ActionName`, while the variables `OS`, `TestName`, and `TestDir` are examples for such values that UFT can retrieve, independent of its running state:

Retrieving the values of built-in variables during runtime is done using code such as the following:

```
Print Environment("ActionIteration")
```

This prints the value of the current `Action` iteration (when runs with input data from the local `DataSheet`). It is possible, of course, to use such variables to control the flow, as is shown in the *Importing an Excel file to a test* recipe in *Chapter 1, Data-driven Tests*.

Built-in variables are read-only.

2. For user-defined variables:

    1. You can define your own `Environment` variables according to the requirements or needs. It is important to keep in mind that, being an object having global scope, the `Environment` object is very useful to store configuration data that is used across tests (for example, website URL, super username and encrypted password, and so on). Though technically feasible, it is not really recommended to use this object as a means to store runtime data that needs to be shared across actions. For that purpose, using a globally defined Dictionary would be much more suitable.

    2. From the **Variable type** list, select **User-defined**. The following screen will be displayed. The main buttons used to edit the variables list (Add, Delete and Edit) are labeled in the following screenshot:

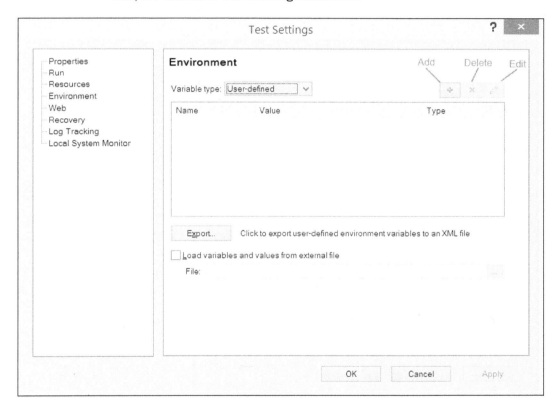

To add, click on the **+** icon. The **Add New Environment Parameter** dialog will pop up. Enter a variable name and value in the appropriate fields, and click on the **OK** button:

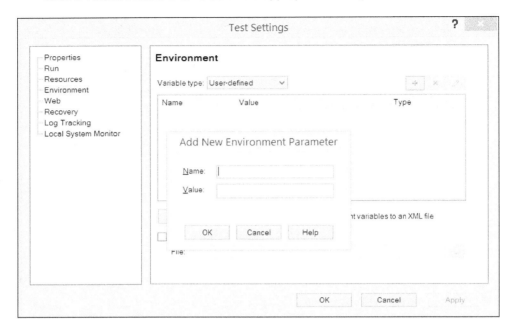

Add two variables, `myvar` and `Myvar`. The next screenshot shows that variable names are case sensitive:

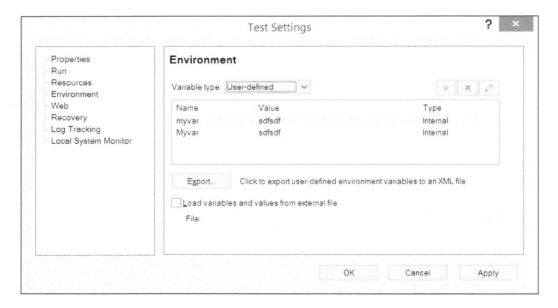

As you can see, the third column labeled **Type** indicates that the variables are Internal. This means that the variables are specific to the current test.

To delete, select the second variable and click on the **x** icon. The following dialog will appear:

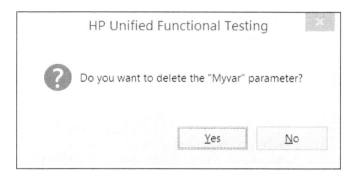

To edit, in order to change the value of a variable, select it and click on the edit icon. The **Edit Environment Parameter** dialog will appear:

Edit the value as per your will and click on **OK** to approve. Your changes will be kept and seen on the variables list in the **Test Settings** dialog.

Though the **Name** field appears to be enabled, it is actually a read-only field. This means that one can only change the value of an Environment variable, not its name. This is important to avoid problems related to existing code, which already refer to previously defined Environment variables. Still, if one wishes to make such a name change, the option of adding a new variable and deleting the old one is always open. Just keep in mind that you may need to make changes to your code.

3. To export:

   1. The **Environment** object can be stored as an XML file. This is useful in order to make general configuration settings available across tests and even test environments or platforms. Click on the **Export** button, select where you want to store the file from the **Save Environment Variable File** dialog that opens, and click on the **Save** button.

4. To import:

   1. As mentioned earlier, it is possible to reuse values previously exported to an XML file. Just mark the checkbox labeled with load variables and values from an external file, and click on the **Browse...** button on the right. Then, select the file from the **Open Environment Variable File** dialog and click on the **Open** button. Please note that for all variables that were loaded from the file, the **Type** column now has the value of External. Consistent with the logic of reusability, these variables cannot be changed from within the **Test Settings** dialog. They are read-only. You can check this by clicking on the edit icon or instead, by using the **Edit Environment Parameter** dialog, you get the **View Environment Parameter** dialog. The fields are both read-only:

It is also possible to import an XML file during runtime. The syntax is as follows:

```
Dim sFilePathname = "C:\Automation\Config\Env_1.xml"

Environment.LoadFromFile sFilePathname
```

Also, if you load it before the test starts to run (using the AOM with an external VBS file, for instance), then the optional Boolean argument, KeepLoaded, is also required:

```
Environment.LoadFromFile sFilePathname, True
```

Otherwise, the variables and values will be lost later.

5. Runtime creation and update:

    1. Though not recommended (as I said, it is better to use a global Dictionary for runtime data sharing), it is technically possible to create user-defined variables during runtime. It is even possible to update their values. These would, of course, disappear from memory when the run is over. The code is—not surprisingly—similar to that of a Dictionary:

        ```
        Environment("MyVarName") = "MyVarValue"
        ```

Do not attempt to change values of built-in or external `Environment` variables. Attempting to do so will result in an error, as shown in the following screenshot:

6. Retrieving values during runtime:

    This can be easily done with code as follows:

    ```
    Print Environment("MyVarName")
    ```

    If the variable does not exist, an error, as shown in the following screenshot, will pop up:

How it works...

The previous section was quite thorough in describing the workings of the `Environment` object, so here we will summarize.

We have seen the main uses of the `Environment` object as a way to define variables that are required during the run session. We have described how to add new persistent variables and delete/edit existing ones using the test settings during design time. We have also explained how, during runtime, one can create new variables and change their values, as well as how to retrieve the values of any **Environment** variable (be it Internal, External, or runtime).

Finally, we discussed the features of Export and Import, stressing that this is how we attain reusability of required configuration variables across tests.

See also

- ▶ Assa, Y. (2008) *Reserved Objects as an Env Object Replacement*, at `http://www.advancedqtp.com/reserved-objects-as-an-env-object-replacement`
- ▶ Vainstein, D. (2008) *Viewing and Editing Environment Complex Parameter Values*, at `http://www.advancedqtp.com/viewing-and-editing-environment-complex-parameter-values/`

Customizing mouse operations (DeviceReplay)

The `DeviceReplay` object enables us to perform mouse and keyboard operations using code, for instance `MouseMove`, `MouseClick`, `PressKey`, `SendString`, and `DragAndDrop`. Though in past years it was not so well documented in HP's materials, now, thanks to the work of some very dedicated people from the QTP (UFT) community, light has been shed upon the workings of this object.

The `DeviceReplay` object is very important for automation, one reason being that the common Test Object methods that UFT provides, such as `Click`, do not always perform well. For example, quite often, one can encounter objects that do not respond to an `onclick` event unless the mouse is actually moved to a location within its bounding rectangle. In such a case, we may revert to the `DeviceReplay` object to override the `Click` method and perform the `MouseMove` operation before sending a `MouseClick` event.

This recipe describes how to use the `DeviceReplay` object to override the `Click` method and perform the `MouseMove` operation before sending a `MouseClick` event.

Getting ready

From the **File** menu, navigate to **New | Test**, or use the *Ctrl + N* shortcut, or open an existing function library.

How to do it...

In the function library, write the following code:

```
Public Function MouseClick_(ByRef obj)
    Dim dr
    Dim X, Y, W, H

    If Not obj.GetROProperty("visible") Then
      MouseClick_ = 1
      Reporter.ReportEvent micWarning, "MouseClick_", _
      "Object is not visible."
      Exit Function
    End If

    With obj
      H = .GetROProperty("height")
      W = .GetROProperty("width")
      X = .GetROProperty("abs_x")
      Y = .GetROProperty("abs_y")
    End With

    If X < 0 Or Y < 0 Then
      MouseClick_ = 1
    Else
      X = X+W\2
      Y = Y+H\2
      Set dr = CreateObject("Mercury.DeviceReplay")
      dr.MouseMove X, Y
      Wait 0, 50
      dr.MouseClick X, Y, 0
      Set dr = Nothing
          MouseClick_ = 0
    End If
  End Function
```

Register the function to the relevant Test Object classes, as shown in the *Registering a method to all classes* recipe (`RegisterUserFunc`) in *Chapter 4, Method Overriding*. For example, we could register the function to the `Click` method of the `Image` class (Web) as follows:

```
RegisterUserFunc "Image", "Click", "MouseClick_"
```

This is done so that, every time we invoke a click event for a Web image, it will first move the mouse to trigger the `onmouseenter` event.

How it works...

The function is generic as it takes an object as an argument. It first checks if the object is visible, which is obligatory to perform a `MouseMove` operation. Then it gets its position and dimensions, to check that it is not positioned out of the screen boundaries (this can happen sometimes with the top-left coordinates being less than zero). If these two checks are passed, then it calculates the middle point of the object, instantiates the `DeviceReplay` object, and moves the mouse to its center. A short delay is added, to ensure that the object reacts to the presence of the mouse within its boundaries, and only then, the `MouseClick` is performed.

Managing processes (SystemUtil)

The `SystemUtil` object is a wrapper that provides a few methods to launch and terminate processes, and to block and unblock user input. In the following sections, we will describe these methods and explain how they work.

Getting ready

From the **File** menu, navigate to **New** | **Test**, or use the *Ctrl + N* shortcut.

How to do it...

Proceed with the following steps:

1. `Run`: It invokes an application with parameters. There is an option to define the work directory, operation, and mode at the opening (maximized and so on). The syntax is as follows:

   ```
   SystemUtil.Run file, [params], [dir], [op], [mode]
   ```

   For example:

   ```
   SystemUtil.Run "iexplore.exe", "google.com",,, 3 'Show maximized
   ```

By `operation` `[op]`, it means which action is to be performed with the file supplied as a string argument with the possible values of open, edit, explore, find, or print. If omitted, the open action is performed. Sending edit with the pathname to a text file will open the default text editor (by default, `Notepad.exe`); explore will open Windows Explorer at the given path; find will open Windows Explorer in search for the files that match the pattern; and finally, print will send the file to the default printer. Of course, correspondingly, if the file is not editable or printable, the statement fails. Using open with a nonexecutable file will open it in its default associated application.

2. `CloseDescendentProcesses`: This closes all processes that were launched by UFT during the run session. It returns the number of processes terminated:

   ```
   SystemUtil.CloseDescendentProcesses()
   ```

3. `CloseProcessByName`: This closes all processes with the name passed as an argument. It returns the number of processes terminated. The syntax is as follows:

   ```
   SystemUtil.CloseProcessByName process_name
   ```

   For example, to close all IE browsers, we may use the following code:

   ```
   i = SystemUtil.CloseProcessByName("iexplore.exe")
   ```

4. `CloseProcessByWndTitle`: This closes all processes that launched windows with the title passed as an argument. It returns the number of processes terminated. The syntax is:

   ```
   SystemUtil.CloseProcessByWndTitle window_title
   ```

   For example, to close a Notepad window with an open file named `MyFile.txt`, we will use the following:

   ```
   i = SystemUtil.CloseProcessByWndTitle("MyFile.txt")
   ```

   To close all notepad windows with `MyFile_` as a prefix in the title and with the additional variable text that follows, we will use a regular expression and indicate that this is the case by sending `True` as a second argument:

   ```
   i = SystemUtil.CloseProcessByWndTitle("MyFile.+\.txt",
     True)
   ```

5. `CloseProcessByHwnd`: It closes a process that launched a window with the handle (hwnd) passed as argument. It returns `true` if found and closed, or `false` otherwise. The syntax is as follows:

   ```
   SystemUtil.CloseProcessByHwnd window_handle
   ```

For example, to close a window for which we know its handle, we will use code similar to the following:

```
SystemUtil.Run "notepad.exe"
hwnd = Window("regexpwndtitle:=.*Notepad").GetROProperty("hwnd")
print hwnd
SystemUtil.CloseProcessByHwnd(hwnd)
```

6. `CloseProcessById`: This closes a process with a specific ID. It returns `true` if found and terminated, or `false` otherwise. The syntax is:

```
SystemUtil.CloseProcessById process_id
```

We can retrieve the process ID for a given window and then terminate its associated process as follows:

```
SystemUtil.Run "notepad.exe"
pid = Window("regexpwndtitle:=.*Notepad").GetROProperty("process
id")
print pid
SystemUtil.CloseProcessById(pid)
```

7. `BlockInput`: This disables the keyboard and mouse for user input during the run session, in order to avoid an accidental interruption by a user. Input is resumed when the run session ends or is paused (for example, runtime error and breakpoint); the *Alt + Ctrl + Del* combination is pressed or else a critical system error will occur. The syntax is as follows:

```
SystemUtil.BlockInput()
```

8. `UnblockInput`: This re-enables the keyboard and mouse for user input during the run session. The syntax is as follows:

```
SystemUtil.UnblockInput()
```

Measuring time (MercuryTimers)

The `MercuryTimers` object enables measurement of time between any two operations. Unlike the native VBScript `Timer` function, the `MercuryTimers` object supports the utilization of multiple `timer_name` time measurement transactions in parallel. In essence, the `Timers` object is a kind of Dictionary that can store different `Timer` objects, each with a unique key. This can be useful to measure the time elapsed at different levels of the run session, and hence, identify possible bottlenecks caused by specific blocks of code.

The `MercuryTimers` object provides the following methods to use with a `Timer` object:

- ▸ `Start`: This starts measuring time in milliseconds
- ▸ `Stop`: This stops measuring time
- ▸ `Continue`: This continues to measure time from the moment the timer stopped
- ▸ `Reset`: This resets the timer to zero.

It also provides the `ElapsedTime` property, which can be used to report, as well as synchronization.

Getting ready

From the **File** menu, navigate to **New** | **Test** or use the *Ctrl + N* shortcut.

How to do it...

Suppose we wish to measure the time taken to perform a complex task, such as a call to a function that validates the data in a Web table. The syntax to instantiate a `Timer` object with the `MercuryTimers` collection is as follows:

```
Set timer_var = MercuryTimers.Timer("timer_name")
```

However, it is possible to instantiate the `Timer` object by simply invoking its `Start` method:

```
MercuryTimers.Timer("timer_name").Start
```

All methods listed previously are used with this syntax.

In the following example, we have added time measurements to the previously discussed procedure to close a process by its ID:

```
MercuryTimers.Timer("Notepad").Start

SystemUtil.Run "notepad.exe"
pID_Notepad = Window("regexpwndtitle:=Notepad").GetROProperty("process
id")

Print MercuryTimers.Timer("Notepad").ElapsedTime

Print pID_Notepad
Print SystemUtil.CloseProcessByid(pID_Notepad)
Print MercuryTimers.Timer("Notepad").ElapsedTime

MercuryTimers.Timer("Notepad").Stop
```

How it works...

As mentioned previously, the `MercuryTimers` object is actually a collection of zero or more `Timer` objects, which we can instantiate during runtime. Each object named `Timer` contributes to the clarity of the code (as opposed to variables using the native VBScript `Timer` function) and work in parallel to the script (asynchronous mode). This means, once we instantiate a `Timer` object and invoke its `Start` method, it works in the background, and the script can continue to run. Using the `ElapsedTime` property, we can check or report the state of affairs. The `Continue`, `Reset`, and `Stop` methods are self-evident and do not require further explanation with regard to their function. However, it is important to note when we might use them. Suppose that we wish to isolate the net time of a function A that calls another auxiliary, function B. We might then wish to start a timer in function A, and stop it just before calling function B (which would have its own timer), then resume the timer in function A after returning from function B.

Resolving file locations (PathFinder)

The `PathFinder` object is useful to find a file or folder in the folders listed in the UFT search list. The method `Locate` returns a string with the path found. Other methods, which are rather undocumented, can be used to manage the list of search folders using code, but they are beyond the scope of this book.

Getting ready

From the **File** menu, navigate to **New | Test**, or use the *Ctrl + N* shortcut. In the **Tools** menu, select **Options**. In the dialog that opens, navigate to **GUI Testing | Folders** and add one folder or more to the search list.

How to do it...

To get the path of a file, use the following syntax:

```
sFilePathname = PathFinder.Locate("MyFile.txt")
```

How it works...

The `PathFinder.Locate` method will search through the folders listed in the search list according to their order and, if found, return the full pathname. It will return the first instance found. This means, if more than one file with the searched name exists in the several folders, the method will proceed based on the priority of the folders.

Loading shared object repositories (RepositoriesCollection)

The `RepositoriesCollection` object provides methods to manage the **Shared Object Repositories** (**SOR**) associated with the actions of the test. The following screenshot shows the methods and properties of the `RepositoriesCollection` object:

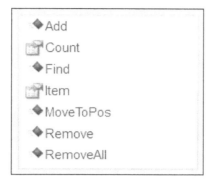

As you might suspect, we can see a recurrent pattern again; the object is very similar to a Dictionary with methods such as `Add`, `Remove`, `RemoveAll`, and the properties `Count` and `Item`. All methods and properties operate in the context of the current action accordingly:

- ▸ The `Add` and `Remove` methods actually add and remove an SOR to and from the `RepositoriesCollection` object, respectively
- ▸ The `RemoveAll` method removes all SORs associated with the current action
- ▸ The `MoveToPos` method changes the priority order of an SOR (that is, its index in the collection)
- ▸ The `Find` method returns the index of a repository within the collection

Getting ready

From the **File** menu, navigate to **New** | **Test**, or use the *Ctrl* + *N* shortcut. Open the Notepad application and add objects to an SOR (not the local OR) by using the Object Repository Manager. Save the SOR in a folder of your choice.

How to do it...

In the `Action` object of the test, write the following code (replace the path with your own):

```
RepositoriesCollection.Add "C:\Temp\Repository1.tsr"

ExitTest
```

Before running the test, the solution explorer will look like the following screenshot, showing only the `Local` OR in the repositories collection:

Insert a breakpoint on the line with the `ExitTest` statement (select it and press *F9*) and then run the test. The run session will pause on that line. Now, watch the **Solution Explorer** window. It should look similar to this:

Notice the lead node with `Repository.tsr` and also the SOR we wanted to load.

Now, press *F10* or *F5*, and watch the **Solution Explorer** window as the test ends. It is restored back to its initial state without the dynamically loaded SOR.

How it works...

The `RepositoriesCollection` object is a kind of Dictionary that can load SORs dynamically and thus, associate them with the current action. The important point to make here refers to when such a feature would be useful, as opposed to the static association of SORs, which is a more common practice. The answer to this question is simple. If the requirements from the automation team/developer include supporting multiple versions of an application, then the `RepositoriesCollection` object would be very useful. For example, we may use an SOR for each version and load it dynamically at the start of the test according to the application version (which can be taken from an `Environment` variable or another source).

Loading and creating XML documents (XMLUtil)

The `XMLUtil` object is a utility that provides methods to do the following:

- Create an XML wrapper
- Load an existing XML file to an XML wrapper

Similar to other wrapper classes provided by UFT (such as those for Test Objects), it is convenient to simplify the usage of XML data via code. It provides an array of methods that cover the most frequently used functions of `XMLDOM`. Of course, if one needs specific functions not provided by the wrapper, it is always possible to recur to the `XMLDOM` or `LINQ` object model (which is not covered in this book).

For example, to get a specific node by ID, we shall use the native method `GetElementByID`.

Getting ready

From the **File** menu, navigate to **New | Test**, or use the *Ctrl + N* shortcut.

How to do it...

In the `Action` object of the test, write the following code:

```
Set xml = XMLUtil.CreateXML()
```

The `xml` variable is set to a new instance of the `MicXmlData` class (see a more detailed description in the following screenshot). The instance will be empty with regard to data. To create an instance with data from an XML file, use code such as the following:

```
Set xml = XMLUtil.CreateXMLFromFile(XMLFilePathname)
```

Where `XMLFilePathname` is a variable containing the full path to an XML file.

The following screenshot shows a partial list of the methods of the `MicXmlData` object that can be used to load and manipulate XML documents:

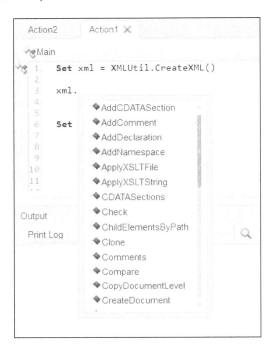

For example, it is possible to use a `MicXmlData` object to create an XML document. During runtime, add data on the go, as it is retrieved from the AUT, and later, load an XML file storing the expected results data and perform a comparison. It is true that in general, an Excel file serving as a `DataTable` would just do. However, if the data needs to be structured in a more complex fashion, then an XML document is more suitable.

Drawing a rectangle on the screen with Win32 API methods (Extern)

In this recipe, you will also see an example of how to use the `Extern` reserved object to define references to methods in external DLLs such as those of the Win32 API. These methods can then be loaded and executed during runtime. We have already seen an example of this in the *Reading values from an INI file* recipe in *Chapter 1, Data-driven Tests*. Here, we will learn how to implement a function that draws a rectangle on the screen with the color of your choice. This is useful to mark areas on the screen that are of interest (especially when the test fails) and hence, makes the report analysis task more efficient.

Getting ready

From the **File** menu, navigate to **New** | **Test**, or use the *Ctrl + N* shortcut.

To complete this recipe, we need the global `Extern` object, which, with proper use, provides UFT with access to the methods of an external **Dynamic Link Library** (**DLL**). We will define a variable and assign it a reference to the global `Extern` object (this is done to avoid persistence, as `Extern` is a reserved object that is not released from memory until UFT closes):

```
Dim oExternObj

Set oExternObj = Extern
```

Then, we will declare the methods required to accomplish our task; in this case, to draw a rectangle on the screen:

```
With oExternObj
    .Declare micHwnd, "GetDesktopWindow", "User32.DLL",
      "GetDesktopWindow"
    .Declare micULong, "GetWindowDC", "User32.DLL", "GetWindowDC",
      micHwnd
    .Declare micInteger, "ReleaseDC", "User32.DLL", "ReleaseDC",
      micHwnd, micULong
    .Declare micULong, "CreatePen", "Gdi32.DLL", "CreatePen",
      micInteger, micInteger, micDword
    .Declare micInteger, "SetROP2", "Gdi32.DLL", "SetROP2",
      micULong, micInteger
    .Declare micULong, "SelectObject", "Gdi32.DLL",
      "SelectObject", micULong, micULong
    .Declare micULong, "DeleteObject", "Gdi32.DLL",
      "DeleteObject", micULong
    .Declare micULong, "GetStockObject", "Gdi32.DLL",
      "GetStockObject", micInteger
    .Declare micULong, "Rectangle", "Gdi32.DLL", "Rectangle",
      micULong, micInteger, micInteger, micInteger, micInteger
End With
```

How to do it...

After we define the connection to the DLL with its returned value and arguments, we will write a function that accepts the following arguments, namely, `TestObject` and a reference to the `Extern` object named `oExternLocal`:

```
Function DrawRect(ByRef TestObject, ByVal oExternLocal)
    Dim YTop, XLeft, YBottom, XRight
    Dim hDC, hPen
```

```
            'Get object coordinates
            With TestObject
                XLeft = .GetROProperty("abs_x")
                YTop = .GetROProperty("abs_y")
                YBottom = YTop+.GetROProperty("height")-1
                XRight = XLeft+.GetROProperty("width")-1
            End With

            With oExternLocal
                ' Get the Desktop DC
                hDC = .GetWindowDC(.GetDesktopWindow)
                ' Create a five pixels wide Pen
                hPen = .CreatePen(6, 5, RGB(0, 0, 0)) ' PS_INSIDEFRAME, 3
                  , RGB(0, 0, 0)
                .SetROP2 hDC, 6 ' hDC, R2_NOT
                .SelectObject hDC, hPen
                ' Use an empty fill
                .SelectObject hDC, .GetStockObject (5) ' NULL_BRUSH

                ' Draw the rectangle
                 .Rectangle hDC, XLeft, YTop, XRight, YBottom

                ' CleanUp
                .ReleaseDC .GetDesktopWindow, hDC
                .DeleteObject hPen
            End With

            Set oExtern = Nothing
        End Function
```

To utilize the function, use the following code:

```
    DrawRect Window("Notepad").WinEditor("Edit"), oExternObj
```

As a result of running the test, the **Notepad** window would look similar to the following screenshot for a brief time (it is possible to extend it by adding a `Wait` command before releasing the drawing context and pen objects):

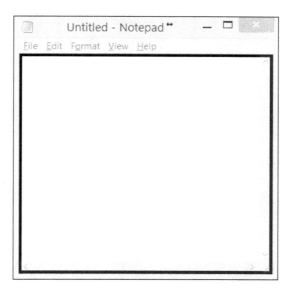

How it works...

First, we use the variable `oExternObj` as a reference (shallow copy) to the `Extern` reserved object to avoid persistence, that is, to ensure that the declared external methods do not remain in memory. Otherwise, we will need to close and reopen UFT to reset the `Extern` object.

Second, we call the function `DrawRect` and pass `TestObject` to be highlighted (in this case, the Notepad `WinEditor`) and the `oExternObj` variable.

Third, the function `DrawRect` calculates the boundaries of the given `TestObject`, and calls the relevant methods from the external Win32 API via the `oExternLocal` object to set the required resources (`Pen`, `Drawing Context`, and so on). It then uses the `Rectangle` method to actually draw a five-pixel-wide rectangle around `TestObject`. Finally, it releases the resources.

Verifying binary file contents (FileCompare)

UFT offers a file-comparison utility that can be used as a COM object; exactly like the `DeviceReplay`, as we have seen earlier in this chapter. This utility is extremely useful to compare pictures and other files storing binary data, by means of calling its `IsEqualBin` method, the syntax being as follows:

```
obj.IsEqualBin FilePathname1, FilePathname2, plErrorCode As
tagCompError, [pFlags As Long]
```

Where `obj` is an instance of `Mercury.FileCompare`, and `plErrorCode` with value 0 (`FC_NO_ERROR`) indicates an **in file compare class showing no error**, and `pFlags` is an optional argument, which, with value 1 (`FC_DIFF_SIZE`), indicates an **in file compare class showing difference of size**.

Getting ready

From the **File** menu, navigate to **New** | **Test**, or use the *Ctrl + N* shortcut.

How to do it...

Write the following code in `Action` of your test:

```
Dim FileComparisonUtil

Set FileComparisonUtil = CreateObject("Mercury.FileCompare")

'Compare two binary files (e.g., pictures)
Print FileComparisonUtil.IsEqualBin(ExpectedFile, ActualFile, 0, 1)
```

How it works...

We simply pass to the function the paths of the files to be compared, and the utility does the work for us, returning `True` if they are equal and `False` otherwise.

Implementing a custom reserved object

UFT can be extended with additional custom reserved objects. This is a feature that can be exploited to develop objects that are instantiated at the UFT's launch time, making the developer's work much more efficient and the code more concise. In this section, we will describe how to implement `GlobalDictionary`, which is to be used for data sharing among different `Actions`.

How to do it...

Proceed with the following steps:

1. In Windows, navigate to **Start | Run**. Type `regedit.exe` and press *Enter*.

2. In **Registry Editor**, search for the folder `ReservedObjects`. It should appear at `HKEY_CURRENT_USER\Software\Mercury Interactive\QuickTest Professional\MicTest\ReservedObjects\`.

3. Add a new key and name it `GlobalDictionary`.

4. Add the following values to the key:

   ❑ `ProgID` of type REG_SZ (string value). Assign it the value of `Scripting.Dictionary`.

   ❑ `UIName` of type REG_SZ (string value). Assign it the value of `GlobalDic`.

   ❑ `VisibleMode` of type REG_DWORD (32-bit value). Assign it the value of 2 (Hexadecimal: 0x00000002).

5. The **Registry Editor** window should look as follows:

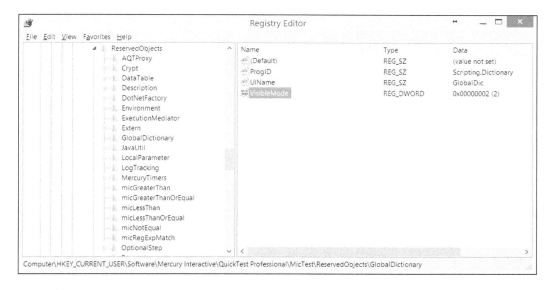

6. Open UFT, and from the **File** menu, navigate to **New | Test**, or use the *Ctrl + N* shortcut.

7. In `Action`, type `GlobalDic.`:

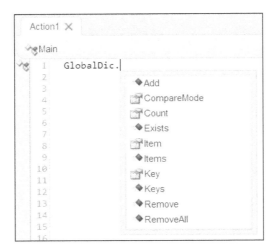

As you can see, UFT now recognizes `GlobalDic` in the same fashion as other reserved objects (for example, `SystemUtil`). The `GlobalDictionary` parameter (`GlobalDic` is the `UIName` we defined in the registry) is already loaded and available, and we also have autocomplete for the syntax of the object methods and properties.

How it works...

UFT takes the definitions of the reserved objects to be loaded from the Windows registry at the `ReservedObjects` key (as mentioned previously). We defined the `progID` (the unique identifier for the COM object) as `Scripting.Dictionary`, which is the `UIName` to be recognized in the UFT editor, and assigned 2 to `VisibleMode` (meaning that it should be visible). When UFT is launched, it loads our custom object, together with the other default objects, and it stays in memory until UFT is closed.

Using remote objects

Working with function libraries can become quite tedious, as each test must have them associated. Deployment issues may arise when tests are copied to other machines. For instance, resources may be missing due to misconfiguration (for example, undefined search paths).

If we could store the code on a server, so that associating function libraries would not be necessary, we would gain three main benefits:

- ▸ Code maintenance and deployment would be simplified and hence become more efficient
- ▸ The dependency of tests on the association of function libraries would vanish
- ▸ Tests would run on any machine that has Internet connectivity and thus reach the code server

In this recipe, we will examine a clever way to accomplish this.

Getting ready

From the **File** menu, navigate to **New | Test**, or use the _Ctrl + N_ shortcut. Create a new file named CROWrapper.wsc (C stands for class and RO for remote object).

 A **Windows Script Component** (**WSC**) file is actually a special XML file that can store components and packages written in various languages that are supported by the **Windows Script Host** (**WSH**).

How to do it...

Write the following code in the component (wsc) file:

```
<?xml version="1.0"?>
-<component id="CROWrapper">
<?component error="true" debug="true"?>
 <registration classid="{D11841E9-B794-4627-AEE6-CA552DFF11C8}"
  version="1" progid="CTOWrapper" description="Wraps methods"/> -
    <public> -<method name="PrintMe"> <parameter
      description="text" name="str"/> </method> </public> -
        <script language="VBScript">
<![CDATA[ Function PrintMe(str) msgbox "In WSC file!!! - " & str
  End Function ]]>
 </script> </component>
```

Store the file on a remote machine (upload to a server). For the purpose of this demonstration, the file can be found at:

http://www.advancedqtp.com/COM/CROWrapper.wsc

Now, write the following code in your test:

```
Const rootURL = "script:http://www.advancedqtp.com/COM/"

Dim oROWrapper

Set oROWrapper = GetObject(rootURL&"CROWrapper.wsc")

Call oROWrapper.PrintMe("Hello")

Set oROWrapper = Nothing
```

Run the test. A message box like the following should appear:

In WSC file!!! - Hello

OK

How it works...

Basically, a component defined in a `wsc` file is equivalent to a class. The statement `Set oROWrapper = GetObject(rootURL&""CROWrapper.wsc"")` actually instantiates the component, so we now have an object of type `CROWrapper`. As such, we can call its public methods, as we would with any object. Note that, as mentioned previously, this means that we can actually use code stored in a server without having to associate it with the test.

Utility statements

UFT uses VBScript as its programming language, but it also has a wide array of commands that are very useful for various purposes, such as flow control. In this section, we shall provide a list of commonly used commands and some others, which the authors think are useful, accompanied by examples and explanations.

Getting ready

From the **File** menu, navigate to **New** | **Test**, or use the *Ctrl + N* shortcut.

How to do it...

Proceed with the following steps:

1. `DescribeResult`: This returns a text description of the specified error code. For example, to print the description of the last runtime error, use:

   ```
   Print DescribeResult(GetLastError())
   ```

2. `ExecuteFile`: This is used to execute the VBScript code in a file (function library) during runtime. This means, instead of associating a function library to your test during design time via the UFT GUI (via **File | Settings | Resources**), you can call it directly using the following syntax:

   ```
   ExecuteFile FilePathname
   ```

3. After the statement is executed, all the definitions (variables, constants, functions, subroutines, and classes) in the file are available from the global scope of the action's script. It is, however, one of the very few statements that are highly recommended as not to be used. The risk is obvious; loading code in such a fashion might cause runtime errors (in the best case) or data overriding (in the worst case). For example, if an identifier (variable, constant, function, and so on) has already been loaded, then an error would arise, as duplicate definitions are not allowed in the same namespace. A worse scenario is if a global variable is reinitialized (assigned with a new value), thus exposing the test to unreliable results.

4. `ExitAction`: This is used to abort the execution of the current action. If the action is set to run for multiple iterations, the consequent iterations will not be executed. Control returns to the calling `Action` (for nested Actions) or to the next `Action`. If `Action` is the last to be run, then the test will stop.

5. `ExitActionIteration`: This is used to abort the execution of the current iteration of an action. When an `Action` is set to run for multiple iterations, control returns to the next iteration (the beginning of the `Action` script). If the iteration is the last, control returns to the calling `Action` (for nested actions) or to the next `Action`. If the `Action` is the last to be run, then the test will stop.

6. `ExitTest`: This is used to abort the execution of the current test. If the test (or the current `Action`) is set to run for multiple iterations, the consequent iterations will not be executed.

7. `ExitTestIteration`: This is used to abort the execution of the current test iteration. When a test is set to run for multiple iterations, control returns to the next iteration (the beginning of the first `Action` script of the test). If the iteration is the last, then the test will stop.

8. `GetLastError`: This is used to retrieve the last VBScript runtime error code (`Long Integer`). See the previous example with `DescribeResult`.

9. `InvokeApplication`: This is obsolete; it is used to invoke an executable file. Use instead, the `SystemUtil.Run` method (see the previous sections in this chapter). The syntax is as follows:

```
InvokeApplication "iexplore.exe"
```

10. `LoadAndRunAction`: This is used to execute a reusable `Action` during runtime, without previously inserting a call and hence, associating it with the test. The syntax is similar to the `RunAction` statement, with one difference—one must supply the path of the test in which `Action` is stored:

```
LoadAndRunAction TestPath, ActionName, [iterations], [parameters]
```

11. The only advantage of this statement is that it enables a more flexible test flow. For example, one can envision that a mechanism within the name of the next action is determined based on the current context, namely, the result of a process and so on. Again, it is one of the very few statements that is highly recommended as not to be used. The risk is obvious, as was with the `ExecuteFile` statement; loading an `Action` in such a fashion exposes the run session to the risks of missing resources, such as an SOR, function library, or `DataSheet`.

12. `OptionalStep`: This is used to define a statement, which does not reflect in the results if it fails to execute. It is only to be used together with Test Objects, as shown in the following example:

```
OptionalStep.Dialog("Confirm Save
  As").WinButton("Yes").Click
```

This will try to click on the **Yes** button of **Dialog Confirm Save As**, but if the object does not exist, the test will continue to run, and no error message will be displayed.

13. `Print`: This is used to print messages, such as values of variables and so on, to the output pane. The syntax is as follows:

```
Print "MyString"

Print StringVariable
```

14. `RegisterUserFunc`: This is used to override Test Object methods. See the *Overriding a Test Object method* recipe (`RegisterUserFunc`) in *Chapter 4, Method Overriding*.

15. `RunAction`: This is used to launch the execution of an `Action`, whether internal or external to the test. If external, it must have association with the test beforehand using the add `Call` to `Action` via the UFT GUI. To launch the execution of unlinked reusable actions, see `LoadAndRunAction`. The syntax is as follows:

```
RunAction "Action2", "1-4", [param1, param2, …, param3]
SetLastError 9 'Assigns 9 to the runtime Err.Number
```

16. `UnregisterUserFunc`: This is used to remove the override from Test Object methods. See the *Overriding a Test Object method* recipe (`RegisterUserFunc`) in *Chapter 4, Method Overriding*.

17. `Wait`: This is used to slow down the script execution. It is recommended to use synchronization points with `WaitProperty` and `Exist`, because the wait time is not specific, and the script would still face the risk of failure. The syntax is as follows:

```
Wait seconds, milliseconds
```

9
Windows Script Host

In this chapter, we will cover the following recipes:

- ► Reading a key from the Windows® system registry
- ► Writing a key to the Windows® system registry
- ► Deleting a key from the Windows® system registry
- ► Running a process using the Windows® system shell

Introduction

Windows Script Host (**WSH**), as the name suggests, is the underlying infrastructure offered by Microsoft Windows® to execute scripts written in a variety of programming (scripting) languages such as VBScript and JavaScript. This infrastructure can be used for a variety of important tasks, such as accessing networks and remote machines, manipulating the registry, and running remote scripts.

This chapter describes a few basic practical uses of WSH that are relevant to test automation. It is not intended to be an exhaustive tutorial or a replacement for Microsoft documentation on the topic.

Reading a key from the Windows® system registry

Reading registry keys and values is an important task. For example, it can assist us in testing the correctness of an application installation process, or in reading specific settings of applications or even operating system environment variables. In this recipe, we will see how to read the value of a key from the registry, specifically the **Java Options** environment variable.

Getting ready

From the **File** menu, navigate to **New** | **Test** or use the *Ctrl + N* shortcut.

How to do it...

The syntax to retrieve the value of a registry key is as follows:

```
Registry_ReadKey
```

Here, `object` is an instance of the `Wscript.Shell` class and `sKeyPath`, a valid key.

An example of how to retrieve the value of the `_JAVA_OPTIONS` environment variable is as shown in the following code snippet:

```
Dim oWshShell, sKeyVal, sKeyPath, sKeyExpected

sKeyPath = "HKEY_CURRENT_USER\Environment\_JAVA_OPTIONS"
Set oWshShell = CreateObject("Wscript.Shell")
sKeyVal = oWshShell.RegRead(sKeyPath)

Print sKeyVal

Set oWshShell = Nothing
```

We can verify the correctness of the retrieved value using a simple conditional structure (assuming that the expected value appears in the action's local datasheet):

```
sKeyExpected = DataTable("Expected_Key", dtLocalSheet)

If sKeyVal <> sKeyExpected Then
Reporter.ReportEvent micFail, "Registry Verification", _
"Actual Key: " & sKeyVal &" differs from Expected Key: "& _
sKeyExpected
End If
```

> The Windows OS stores the names and values of its environment variables (not to be confused with UFT's environment variables) under the registry key HKEY_CURRENT_USER\Environment.

How it works...

We simply create an instance of the `WScript.Shell` class, and use the `RegRead` method to retrieve the value of a valid registry key.

Writing a key to the Windows® system registry

The purpose of writing registry keys and values is so that they can be used within automated tests. The reason is that, in general, automation should refrain from making changes to the operating system, and this includes the registry. This is necessary to keep our automated tests as less invasive as possible. However, it is important to know how this can be accomplished.

To write a value to a custom registry key that passes UFT data gathered by a process running in parallel to the automated test, UFT uses the `RegRead` method at the appropriate time to retrieve the data. This allows, in parallel, the asynchronous usage of the testing tool and external executables.

In this recipe, we will see how to write a custom key to the registry.

Getting ready

From the **File** menu, navigate to **New** | **Test**, or use the *Ctrl + N* shortcut. You can use the same test as in the previous recipe.

How to do it...

The syntax to write the value of a registry key is as follows:

```
object.RegWrite sKeyPath, sKeyVal, sKeyType
```

Here, `object` is an instance of the `Wscript.Shell` class, and `sKeyPath` a valid key.

An example of how to write a new custom string (`REG_SZ`) type key is shown using the following code snippet:

```
Dim oWshShell, sKeyPath, sKeyVal, sKeyType

sKeyPath = "HKEY_CURRENT_USER\MyCustomKey\MyCustomData\MyValue"
sKeyVal = "This is a UFT made registry key"
sKeyType = "REG_SZ"

Set oWshShell = CreateObject("Wscript.Shell")
oWshShell.RegWrite sKeyPath, sKeyVal, sKeyType

sKeyVal = oWshShell.RegRead(sKeyPath)

Print sKeyVal

Set oWshShell = Nothing
```

How it works...

We simply create an instance of the `WScript.Shell` class and use the `RegWrite` method to write the value of our custom registry key. We then use `RegRead` to print the value to the output pane.

Deleting a key from the Windows® system registry

Automated tests rarely delete registry keys and values. However, in some cases (such as in the case described in the previous recipe), deleting the custom key would be a reasonable cleaning procedure. In this recipe, we will see how to do it.

Getting ready

From the **File** menu, navigate to **New** | **Test**, or use the *Ctrl + N* shortcut. You can use the same test as in the previous recipe.

How to do it...

The syntax to delete the value of a registry key is as follows:

```
object.RegDelete sKeyPath
```

Here, `object` is an instance of the `Wscript.Shell` class and `sKeyPath` a valid key.

For example, to delete the new custom string (REG_SZ) type key we created in the previous recipe, use the following code snippet:

```
Dim oWshShell, sKeyPath, sKeyName, sKeyVal, sKeyType

sKeyPath = "HKEY_CURRENT_USER\MyCustomKey\MyCustomData\MyValue"

Set oWshShell = CreateObject("Wscript.Shell")
oWshShell.RegDelete sKeyPath

Set oWshShell = Nothing
```

How it works...

We simply create a WScript.Shell object and use the RegDelete method to delete the value of our custom registry key.

Running a process using the Windows® system shell

In *Chapter 8, Utility and Reserved Objects,* we described the SystemUtil object and learned how to open an application using the Run method. In this recipe, we will describe how to accomplish the same by using the Wscript.Shell object.

Getting ready

From the **File** menu, navigate to **New | Test**, or use the *Ctrl + N* shortcut. You can use the same test as in the previous recipe.

How to do it...

The syntax to run an application (or an external script) is as follows:

```
object.Run sApplicationPath, [intWindowStyle], [bWaitOnReturn]
```

Here, object is an instance of the Wscript.Shell class, and sApplicationPath is a valid application path. The intWindowStyle (refer to the following table) and bWaitOnReturn variables (True/False) are optional. By default, the script does not wait until the external application finishes and returns 0.

The following table enumerates the possible values of `intWindowStyle` (this is sourced from the Help file on the Microsoft Windows Scripting Technologies website):

Value	Description
0	This hides the current window and activates another window.
1	This value activates and displays a window. If the window is minimized or maximized, the system restores it to its original size and position. An application should specify this flag when displaying the window for the first time.
2	This value activates the window and displays it as a minimized window.
3	This value activates the window and displays it as a maximized window.
4	This value displays a window in its most recent size and position. The active window remains active.
5	This value activates the window and displays it in its current size and position.
6	This value minimizes the specified window and activates the next top-level window in the Z order.
7	This value displays the window as a minimized window. The active window remains active.
8	This value displays the window in its current state. The active window remains active.
9	This value activates and displays the window. If the window is minimized or maximized, the system restores it to its original size and position. An application should specify this flag when restoring a minimized window.
10	This value sets the show state based on the state of the program that started the application.

For example, to open the Notepad application, use the following code snippet:

```
Dim oWshShell, sApp

sApp = "notepad.exe"
Set oWshShell = CreateObject("Wscript.Shell")

oWshShell.Run sApp

Set oWshShell = Nothing

ExitTest
```

How it works...

We simply create an instance of the `WScript.Shell` class and use the `Run` method to invoke an application of our choice (in this case, Notepad).

10
Frameworks

In this chapter, we will cover:

- ▶ Introduction to test automation frameworks
- ▶ Designing a test automation framework
- ▶ Building a test controller
- ▶ Building a reusable component (action)
- ▶ Building an event handler
- ▶ Building a test reporter

Introduction to test automation frameworks

This section intends to cover:

- ▶ Definition of a test automation framework
- ▶ Advantages of using a test automation framework
- ▶ Types of test automation frameworks (modular-driven, data-driven, keyword-driven, model-driven, and hybrid)
- ▶ Designing a test automation framework

Definition of a test automation framework

Test automation framework (often referred to in the testing industry as testware automation frameworks) is an integrated software solution that defines the rules for the development, maintenance, and execution of **automated test assets**. Typically, such a solution also defines how test results are reported, how runtime errors are handled, and how test data is managed. A test automation framework comprises function libraries, data sources (for example, Excel or XML files and DB), object models (such as stored in an object repository), and it may also include additional reusable external modules (for example, DLL files, COM objects, configuration scripts, and so on).

Advantages of using a test automation framework

A well-designed test automation framework typically contributes towards lower reduce development and maintenance costs of automated test assets. This means that, ideally, a framework should use generic and agnostic design patterns to provide a solution that is relevant, effective, maintainable, efficient, manageable, portable, reliable, and diagnosable.

The preceding list is not meant to be exhaustive, but provides the main features that are expected from a robust automation framework.

Another aspect of test automation that is quite often neglected, but one that can make a great contribution to design patterns, is the **command wrapper** (used when implementing test procedures and functions). This will also be explained later in this section.

Types of test automation frameworks

There are several generic types of test automation frameworks' design patterns:

- Modular-driven framework
- Data-driven framework
- Keyword-driven framework
- Model-driven framework (for example, **Action Based Testing** (**ABT**) or as termed in UFT, **Business Process Testing** (**BPT**))
- Hybrid approach framework

 Hybrid approach is a term used by the authors that refers to test automation frameworks that are a combination of the other design patterns, usually such that, they implement a blend of all, or part of, the design feature of the other patterns.

Selecting a framework type

As far as which framework type to select is concerned, it depends on the requirements we have to meet and the level of automation maturity required. No single pattern type is a silver bullet, and a more complex framework should not be used if the additional complexity is not expected to yield significant added value. We shall now define and explain the different patterns mentioned earlier.

Modular-driven framework

A modular-driven pattern uses classes and objects to encapsulate all the entities involved in the automation project. Basically, a modular-driven pattern can be considered a particular case of the hybrid approach. This is because the utilization of classes and objects is typically also accompanied by the usage of the features of the keyword-driven pattern (in more complex implementations) and the data-driven pattern.

Using classes (as described in detail in the previous chapters) allows for a better organized code base, typically resulting in a more concise, clearer, as well as more flexible, extensible, and, maintainable code. This also enables us to use object-oriented design patterns to maximize reusability and enhance the performance of our test suites. For example, a typical modular-driven pattern has a well-defined structure (or template) to implement runnable processes using the command wrapper pattern (refer to *Chapter 7, Using Classes*). This, in turn, simplifies the way data is loaded, saved, and shared; the way events are reported to the log file; how the flow is controlled; and finally, the way exceptions are handled.

Data-driven frameworks

A data-driven pattern supports test iterations and flow branching according to external input data. UFT can, by default, offer such a framework out-of-the-box; all we have to do is define the parameters in the DataTable, retrieve the values of these in our code where appropriate, and set the test or Action iterations (datasheet rows range) we wish to execute (refer to *Chapter 1, Data-driven Tests*).

Keyword-driven frameworks

A keyword-driven pattern is also a data-driven pattern, but with another level of abstraction; commands are encapsulated as data entities (keywords) and mapped to actual functions implemented in code.

These keywords are listed in their planned order of execution in some kind of data source (for instance, Excel worksheet, XML file, or DB). Typically, this data source would also include the corresponding parameter values for each operation. A central mechanism, often referred to as a controller or parser, reads the sequence of keywords and invokes the procedures associated with them.

Central to a keyword-driven pattern is the desire to provide nontechnical test engineers, who do not possess coding skills, with the ability to implement **automated test scenarios** (also referred to as test scripts) using a high-level structured language composed with words that represent underlying coded processes of varying complexity.

This pattern is very popular, and its main advantages are:

- Automation test scenarios are represented by steps composed of basic building blocks (procedures) and parameters.

- Apart from more complex cases, which are difficult to capture with a simple step-by-step representation, coding is essentially not required to automate the tests.

- Different levels of granularity are supported. For example, a keyword may represent a single test object method (for instance, `PressOK`) or a procedure (for example, `Login`). The latter is basically ABT or BPT, as the functionality offered by UFT requires connectivity with HP ALM/QC.

A keyword-driven pattern also has some challenges that require our attention. For instance, it typically carries the additional cost of developing a **User Interface** (**UI**) to manage, build, and validate the data entered by the designer of the tests while defining automated test scenarios.

Hybrid frameworks

A hybrid pattern is one that combines some or all the features of the mentioned framework types. It is typically implemented with a strong emphasis on design patterns, to provide a solution that yields high scores in (source Hybrid (keyword/data-driven) frameworks, ANZTB Conference, 2010 by Jonathon Wright):

- Maintainability: significantly reduces the test maintenance effort

- Reusability: due to modularity of test cases and library functions

- Manageability: effective test design, execution, and traceability

- Accessibility: to design, develop & modify tests whilst executing

- Availability: scheduled execution can run unattended on a 24/7 basis

- Reliability: to advanced error handling and scenario recovery

- Flexibility: framework independent of system or environment under test

- Measurability: customizable reporting of test results ensure quality

Designing a test automation framework

Before we start coding, it is important to think carefully about the underlining structure (architecture) of the target framework. This will minimize the costs of framework development and maintenance of the **automated test assets**, so that they can easily be extended to cover new requirements.

Key design activities for a framework

The key activities we need to perform in order to design a robust test automation framework may include:

- Defining a standard project (or solution) folder hierarchy.
- Defining a standard configuration and launcher script. This is typically not required when using HP ALM/QC together with UFT, thanks to their interoperability.
- Designing a standard format for the automation components.
- Designing reusable modules to reduce development and maintenance costs.
- Designing a layered architecture of reusable modules.
- Designing a standard flow control module.
- Designing a standard data storage, loading, and sharing mechanism.
- Designing a standard reporting mechanism.
- Designing a standard error/exception handling mechanism.

Components of a framework

The components of a test automation framework comprise an array of modules that manage different requirements for automation. The main modules include a flow controller, a reporter/logger, and an exception handler. For simplicity, data loading is implemented here using the UFT native DataTable, but of course, other options, such as XML files or a DB, can be used.

We also use a command wrapper design pattern to implement reusable runnable components, which are direct replacements for the reusable UFT actions.

We will now list out the component design patterns.

Controller

The controller supports the following requirements:

▶ Loading the list of reusable components (actions)

▶ Importing the datasheet for each action

▶ Running each action for the number of iterations indicated

▶ Invoking the event handler to check if an error was thrown and handle it as predefined

Reusable components (actions)

A reusable component supports the following requirements:

▶ Implementing the runnable interface (requires a `Run` method to be implemented), which will execute the actual code

▶ Implementing the data loading of its parameters from the DataTable, as required for each iteration

▶ Reporting the results of the Action, using the generic reporting mechanism

Event handler

The event handler supports the following requirements:

▶ Enabling the mapping of a procedure to a key (basically, an error number)

▶ Invoking the corresponding procedure when a key (error number) is passed

▶ Ensuring that the error handling procedures should be implemented as actions

Reporter

The custom reporter supports the following requirements:

▶ Retrieving the data for the report from the sending Action

▶ Invoking the UFT and passing it to the appropriate parameters

To conclude this recipe, the basic design outlined here covers the basic needs of a test automation framework, namely, flow control, reporting, data loading and sharing, and event/exception handling. This design pattern also supports keyword-/data-driven flow control, and encourages the use of highly effective object-oriented design patterns. The next sections will describe in detail how to build each of these components.

Building a test controller

In this recipe, we will see how to build a controller for our test automation framework. As outlined in the previous recipe, the controller will load the list of actions, and for each Action, it will import the corresponding datasheet. For each data-driven iteration, it will initialize the Action and invoke its `Run` method.

Most often, a controller is implemented as a function. Here, we will implement it as a class. The reason is that, this way, we can instantiate a controller during runtime to support dynamic branching of the test flow.

Getting ready

Create a folder structure, as follows:

- `C:\Automation`
- `C:\Automation\Data`
- `C:\Automation\Lib`
- `C:\Automation\Tests`
- `C:\Automation\Config`
- `C:\Automation\Results`
- `C:\Automation\Solutions`

Create a new test and save it as `Framework_MasterDriver` under the subfolder `C:\Automation\Tests`. You can also save the solution under the `Solutions` subfolder. Under the `Data` subfolder, create a subfolder named `Framework_MasterDriver` and create an Excel file named `TestScenario.xls`.

Create a new function library. From the **File** menu, navigate to **New | Function Library...**, or use the *Alt + Shift + N* shortcut. Save the file as `cls.Controller.vbs`.

An Excel file named `TestScenario.xls` with a datasheet named `Steps` is required to be able to use the controller, as shown in the following example:

STEP_ID	ACTION_NAME	RUN	DATASHEET	ITERATIONS	ON_FAILURE
10	OpenApp	TRUE	N/A		ExitTest
20	Login	TRUE			ExitTest
30	Search	TRUE			ExitAction
40	AddToCart	TRUE		1-3	ExitAction

STEP_ID	ACTION_NAME	RUN	DATASHEET	ITERATIONS	ON_FAILURE
50	Checkout	TRUE			ExitAction
60	Logout	TRUE	N/A		ExitAction
70	CloseApp	TRUE	N/A		ExitTest

For each step that is data driven, the Excel file should include a specific datasheet named by the Action name (the name of the class that implements the action. Refer to the *Building a reusable component (action) recipe*. If the ITERATIONS parameter is left empty, then the controller will run only one iteration.

For example, for the AddToCart action, a datasheet named AddToCart is required, and we wish to run it three times as shown in the following datasheet example:

PRODUCT_NAME
My Book 1
My Book 2
My Book 3

It is possible to share datasheets with different actions, by specifying a DATASHEET value that is different from the Action name. If the Action is not data driven, then N/A should be entered.

How to do it...

Proceed with the following steps:

1. Add the following Environment variables to the test (of course, it would be most efficient to export these to an XML file to allow for reusability for all the tests):

   - DATA_FOLDER with the root path value of the folder in which the automation input data is stored. In our case it will be C:\Automation\Data\.

   - ON_FAILURE with the value of the action to be taken if a problem is found. It is used by the ASSERT_RESULT function. It's possible that the values are ExitTest and ExitAction.

2. In the controller function library, cls.Controller.vbs, write the following code:

```
Const C_STR_TEST_SCENARIO_XLS = "TestScenario.xls"

Const C_OBJ_OF_CLASS_MSG = "--- Object of Class "

Const C_OBJ_LOADED_MSG = " was loaded ---"

Const C_OBJ_UNLOADED_MSG = " was unloaded ---"
```

These constants are auxiliary, and they are used to log/report:

```
Class Controller
    Public Status
    Public Details

    Function Run(ByVal strTestSetsPathName)
        ' --------------------------------------------------
        ' Function    :    Run
        ' Purpose     :    Runs the steps (procedures
            implemented as Command Wrappers)
        ' Args        :    ByVal strTestSetsPathName
        ' Returns     :    0 on success; 1 on failure
        ' --------------------------------------------------
        ' Usage       :    Run("C:\Automation\Test_Sets\")
        ' Notes       :    1) Uses a Local DataSheet to
            control the steps flow
        '                  2) Uses GetClassInstance
        '                  3) Uses CNum
        '                  4) Uses ASSERT_RESULT
        '                  5) Uses GetIterations
        '                  6) Uses PrintReportInfo
        '                  7) Uses GetNormalizedStatus
        '                  8) Uses Timestamp
        ' --------------------------------------------------
        Const C_STEPS_DATASHEET = "Steps"
        Dim iTestStatus, iStepStatus, iIterationStatus
            'Statuses at all levels of flow control

        Dim dt, rowcount 'Datasheet with the steps list
        Dim bExitAction, bExitTest, bRun, iStep, iter,
            oAction, sActionName 'For the steps and
            iterations flow control
        Dim arrIterations 'To support iterations
        Dim sFolder, sDatasheet 'For datasheet import
        ' --------------------------------------------------


        ' --------------------------------------------------
        '--- Get the name of the folder from which to
            import datasheets (same as test)
        sFolder = Environment("TestName")
        '--- Add sheet
        DataTable.AddSheet(C_STEPS_DATASHEET)
        '--- Import steps datasheet
```

```
Call DataTable.ImportSheet(strTestSetsPathName &
  "\" & sFolder &"\" & C_STR_TEST_DATA_XLS,
  C_STEPS_DATASHEET, C_STEPS_DATASHEET)

Set iTestStatus     = [As Num](0)
Set dt              =
  DataTable.GetSheet(C_STEPS_DATASHEET)
rowcount            = dt.GetRowCount
bExitTest           = False

PrintReportInfo "Test " & Environment("TestName"),
  "Started at " & Timestamp()
```

Until this point we had some initialization commands. Now, comes the main `For` loop that manages the run session:

```
'--- Loop on all steps defined in the datasheet
    For iStep = 1 To rowcount
        bExitAction = False
        dt.SetCurrentRow(iStep)
        sActionName =
          dt.GetParameter("ACTION_NAME").Value
        bRun = dt.GetParameter("RUN").Value
```

Within the loop, we initialize the flag `bExitAction`, set the row in the `Steps` datasheet, and retrieve the name of the current action. We also get the value of the `RUN` parameter, which is used to check if the current Action is planned for execution.

```
'--- Check if the step is planned to be executed
        If CStr(bRun) = "TRUE" Then
            '--- Get an instance of the sActionName class
            ASSERT_RESULT(GetClassInstance(oAction, "["
              & sActionName & "]"))
            '--- Reset Step status
            Set iStepStatus    = [As Num](0)
            '--- Assign Step id
            oAction.StepNum =
              dt.GetParameter("STEP_ID").Value
            '--- Get datasheet name to import (for
              data-driven actions)
            sDatasheet =
              dt.GetParameter("DATASHEET").Value
            If Trim(sDatasheet) = "" Then
                sDatasheet = sActionName
            End If
```

```
'--- Check if the Action is data-driven
If sDatasheet <> "N/A" Then
    '--- Import datasheet to local
    Call
      DataTable.ImportSheet
      (strTestSetsPathName
      & "\" & sFolder &"\" &
      C_STR_TEST_DATA_XLS
      , sDatasheet,
      Environment("ActionName"))
    '--- Assign the new sheet to the step
    Set oAction.dt = DataTable.LocalSheet
End If
```

This code uses the ASSERT_RESULT function to ensure that the requested Action is valid (that is, the returned object by GetClassInstance is not equal to Nothing). The iStepStatus variable is initialized as a CNum object (a custom class that enables object-oriented operations such as ++, and –), using the [As Num] method, which acts as the CNum constructor. We then assign the current Action its number (or ID) from the STEP_NUM parameter, and if it is a data-driven action, we assign the Action its corresponding datasheet as well.

```
'--- Get list of iterations (e.g., "1-3,7,13-17") as
  System.Collections.ArrayList and sort
            Set arrIterations =
              GetIterations(dt.GetParameter
              ("ITERATIONS").Value)
            arrIterations.Sort()
            '--- Reset iterations status
            Set iIterationStatus = [As Num](0)
            '--- Send start Step to the log
            PrintReportInfo "Step " & oAction.StepNum &
              " - Action '" & sActionName & "'"
              , "Started at " & Timestamp()
```

We then get the list of rows from which the Action will retrieve its input data. The number of items in the list determines the number of iterations in the Action. Take note that the list of rows can include a mix of single rows and ranges separated by commas. Next, we reach the inner For loop that controls the iterations flow for each action.

This will check if the Action is data driven, and if so, it sets the datasheet row for the current iteration and the Action's Iteration field. Then, it simply invokes the Run method of the Action and gets the status of the iteration.

Note that we use the `On Error Resume Next` directive just before invoking the action's `Run` method, in order to catch any exception and redirect it to `ErrorHandler` (refer to the *Building an event handler* recipe):

```
'--- Loop for each iteration
            For Each iter In arrIterations
                PrintReportInfo "Step " &
                    oAction.StepNum & " - Action '" &
                    sActionName & "'", "Started iteration
                    " & iter & " at " & Timestamp()
                '--- Check if the Action is data-driven
                If sDatasheet <> "N/A" Then
                    '--- Set the row that corresponds
                        to the current iteration
                    oAction.dt.SetCurrentRow(iter)
                End If
                '--- Set the Iteration field of the
                    Action
                oAction.Iteration = iter
                ' ------------------------------------
                    '--- Execute the Action
                ' ------------------------------------
                On Error Resume Next '--- Try
                oAction.Run
                ' ------------------------------------
                If Err.Number <> 0 Then 'Catch
                    me.ErrorHandler.RunMappedProcedure(Err.
                    Number)
                End If
                On Error Goto 0
                ' ------------------------------------
                '--- Get the Action status
                iIterationStatus.[+=]oAction.Status
```

Next, we send the result to the log. The `GetNormalizedStatus` function accepts an integer and checks if it represents success or failure. It is possible to customize such a function, depending on the requirements of the test automation framework. If the status is a failure, then we check with the `Eval` statement as to what we should do, as defined in the `ON_FAILURE` parameter.

For example, if `ExitAction` was set, then the next iteration of the Action will not be run, and the controller will attempt to execute the next Action (of course, one must ensure beforehand that the actions are independent). If the test flow cannot be continued, we can set the value of the ON_FAILURE parameter in the datasheet to `ExitTest`.

```
'--- Send iteration result to the log
            PrintReportInfo "Step " &
              oAction.StepNum & " - Action '" &
              sActionName & "'", "Ended iteration "
              & iter & " at " & Timestamp() & "
              with status " &
              GetNormalizedStatus(iIterationStatus)
        '--- Check the status of the iteration
            If
              GetNormalizedStatus(iIterationStatus)
              > 0 Then
        '--- Evaluate if a failure condition occurred
                Eval("b" &
                  dt.GetParameter("ON_FAILURE") &
                  "=TRUE")
                '--- Check the Exit flags
                If bExitAction Then Exit For
                If bExitTest Then Exit For
            End If
        Next '--- Iteration


    '--- Update the Step status with the iteration
      status
            iStepStatus.[+=]iIterationStatus
    '--- Send Action result (end) to the log
            PrintReportInfo "Step " & oAction.StepNum &
              " - Action '" & sActionName & "'", "Ended
              at " & Timestamp() & " with status " &
              GetNormalizedStatus(iStepStatus)
            '--- Dispose of the oAction object
            Set oAction = Nothing
```

If the Action is not planned to be executed, it is reported to the results so that the person analyzing them will be aware of this fact. If the Action RUN parameter is empty, then the controller will report that it was undefined.

```
        ElseIf CStr(bRun) = "FALSE" Then
                '--- Send skip Step to the log
                PrintReportInfo "Step " &
                    dt.GetParameter("STEP_ID").Value & "
                    - Action '" & sActionName & "'", "Not
                    planned to run"
        Else
            '--- Send no directive for Step to the log
            PrintReportInfo "Step " &
                dt.GetParameter("STEP_ID").Value & " -
                Action '" & sActionName & "'",
                "Undefined"
        End If
```

Next, the iTestStatus variable will be updated with the status of the step (Action), which, as previously indicated, stores the accrued status of its iterations.

The ExitTest flag is checked, and if set, then the main For loop is terminated. The result is sent to the log again and returned by the Run function.

```
'--- Update the Test status with the iteration status
        iTestStatus.[+=]GetNormalizedStatus(iStepStatus)
        '--- Check the Exit flag
        If bExitTest Then Exit For
    Next '--- Step (Action)
    '--- Send Test result (end) to the log
    PrintReportInfo "Test " & Environment("TestName"),
        "Ended at " & Timestamp() & " with status " &
        GetNormalizedStatus(iTestStatus)
    '--- Return status
    Run = GetNormalizedStatus(iTestStatus)
End Function
' --------------------------------------------------
' End: Run
' --------------------------------------------------
End Class
```

3. To use the controller, add the following function in the same library:

```
Function RunTest()
    Dim oTestRunner

    ASSERT_RESULT(GetClassInstance(oTestRunner,
      "Controller"))

    RunTest = oController.Run(Environment("DATA_FOLDER"))
End Function
```

4. The `RunTest` function uses the `GetClassInstance` function to get an instance of the controller. To use it, just write the following line of code in your test (`Action`):

```
ExitTest(RunTest())
```

When the `RunTest` function is invoked, the controller will roll the Actions as described, and its `Run` method will return the status of the test. Finally, the test will exit and the status will be returned.

How it works...

It is quite evident that a test automation framework implementing such a design for the controller module covers most of the requirements for flow control, error handling, reporting, and data loading.

Building a reusable component (action)

The controller was designed to load, configure, and execute **Action Based Testing** (**ABT**) or **Business Process Testing** (**BPT**), which are classes built as command wrappers with a common `Run` method in which the main flow of the Action is implemented. In this section, we will see how to implement such an action.

Getting ready

From the **File** menu, navigate to **New | Function Library...**, or use the *Alt + Shift + N* shortcut. Save the file as `cls.Actions.vbs` in the `C:\Automation\Lib` folder.

How to do it...

As mentioned before, a reusable component (action) is a class that implements the command wrapper design pattern. The following code shows the sample class Login as a typical example for an Action within this framework:

```
Class [Login]
    ' ---------------------------------------------------
    ' Reusable Action: Login
    ' Description: Login to the application
    ' ---------------------------------------------------
    Public Status
    Public Iteration
    Public StepNum
    Public dt
    Public Details

    Public Function Run()
        me.Details = "Ended with "
        me.Status.[=]0
        '---
        me.Status.[+=]EnterUsername()
        me.Status.[+=]EnterPassword()
        me.Status.[+=]ClickOnLoginButton()

        '--- Report
        Call ReportActionStatus(me)
    End Function

    Function EnterUsername()
        EnterUsername =
          me.Parent.WebEdit("txtUsername").Set(dt.
          GetParameter("USERNAME"))
    End Function

    Function EnterPassword()
        EnterPassword =
          me.Parent.WebEdit("txtPassword").Set(dt.
          GetParameter("PASSWORD"))
    End Function
```

```
Function ClickOnLoginButton()
    ClickOnLoginButton = me.Parent.WebButton("btnLogin").Click
End Function

Property Get Parent()
    Set Parent = Browser("MyStore").Page("Main")
End Property

Private Sub Class_Initialize
    Call InfoClassInstance(me, C_OBJ_LOADED_MSG)
    Set me.Status = [As Num](0)
End Sub
Private Sub Class_Terminate
    Call InfoClassInstance(me, C_OBJ_UNLOADED_MSG)
    Set me.Status = Nothing
End Sub
End Class
```

 The Test Objects referred to in the internal methods of the class are for illustration purposes only.

How it works...

The controller creates an instance of the Login class when it finds its name in the Steps datasheet and is planned to run (the RUN parameter equals TRUE).

It then invokes the object's Run method, in which the main flow of the Action is coded. Note that additional fields, functions, subroutines, and properties can be added to extend the basic pattern of an action; thus making it a very powerful and flexible tool to encapsulate basic blocks of code, which are usually business-oriented functions. The Run method finally invokes the ReportActionStatus function, which takes care to send the information accumulated during the process to the UFT reporter.

Note how data is referred to in the internal functions:

```
dt.GetParameter("USERNAME")
```

Through the dt field of the Action, which was set by the controller with a reference to the LocalSheet DataTable, we can retrieve the values of any of the required parameters.

Building an event handler

One risk we must handle during run sessions is exceptions, as they can have a fatal impact on the robustness of our automated tests. UFT provides the recovery scenario as a built-in solution (refer to *Chapter 6, Event and Exception Handling*), but it is quite complex to implement and may hinder the performance of the test.

In this recipe, we will see how to implement a simple recovery mechanism that is integrated with the controller (described previously) and that utilizes the same design pattern used for the regular actions to implement recovery procedures.

Getting ready

Add an Environment variable to the test. Name it `ERR_DEFAULT` and set its value to `StopRunSession`. Add another Environment variable named `ERR_9` and set its value to `ClearError`. Create a function library named `cls.EventHandler.vbs` in the `Lib` folder, as already described in the previous recipe.

How to do it...

The following code shows a sample procedure implemented as an Action. The `StopRunSession` class is used in our framework to handle an exception by stopping the run session, and it is used as default. Write the following code in the `cls.EventHandler.vbs` function library:

```
Class StopRunSession
    ' -----------------------------------------------
    ' Reusable Action: StopRunSession
    ' Description: Stops the run in case of an unhandled
      error/exception
    ' -----------------------------------------------
    Public Status
    Public Iteration
    Public StepNum
    Public dt
    Public Details

    Public Function Run()
        me.Details = "Ended with "
        me.Status.[=]Reporter.RunStatus

        '--- Report
        Call ReportActionStatus(me)
```

```
        '--- Stops the run session
        ExitTest(Reporter.RunStatus)
    End Function

    Private Sub Class_Initialize
        Call InfoClassInstance(me, C_OBJ_LOADED_MSG)
        Set me.Status = [As Num](0)
    End Sub
    Private Sub Class_Terminate
        Call InfoClassInstance(me, C_OBJ_UNLOADED_MSG)
        Set me.Status = Nothing
    End Sub
End Class
```

The procedure was built based on the same command wrapper pattern as the regular reusable Actions. The procedure will be invoked any time by the RunMappedProcedure method (shown in the following code snippet) of the EventHandler class, which will not find a matching procedure for a given error code.

Note that in this sample implementation, the value of the procedure associated with the error number is taken from the environment, but more elaborate design patterns could have been mapped into an XML file or DB:

```
Class EventHandler
    Function RunMappedProcedure(ByVal strError)
        Dim oProcedure

'--- Try to execute the procedure associated with the error (if
   exists)
        If GetClassInstance(oProcedure, Environment("ERR_" &
          CStr(Abs(strError)))) = 0 Then
            RunMappedProcedure = oProcedure.Run
            Exit Function
        End If
'--- Try to execute the default procedure to handle errors (if
   exists)
        If GetClassInstance(oProcedure,
          Environment("DEFAULT_ERROR_HANDLER")) Then
            RunMappedProcedure = oProcedure.Run
            Exit Function
        End If
    End Function
End Class
```

The following code shows another sample procedure implemented as an Action. It is used in our test automation framework to handle a specific exception by clearing the error, and the procedure is mapped to error code number 9 (Subscript out of range). This can be written in the cls.EventHandler.vbs function library file, as follows:

```
Class ClearError
    ' ------------------------------------------------
    ' Reusable Action: ClearError
    ' Description: Clears the error in case of an unhandled
      error/exception
    ' ------------------------------------------------
    Public Status
    Public Iteration
    Public StepNum
    Public dt
    Public Details

    Public Function Run()
        me.Details = "Ended with "
        me.Status.[=]0

        '--- Report
        Call ReportActionStatus(me)

        '--- Clears the error
        Err.Clear
    End Function

    Private Sub Class_Initialize
        Call InfoClassInstance(me, C_OBJ_LOADED_MSG)
        Set me.Status = [As Num](0)
    End Sub
    Private Sub Class_Terminate
        Call InfoClassInstance(me, C_OBJ_UNLOADED_MSG)
        Set me.Status = Nothing
    End Sub
End Class
```

How it works...

When the controller tries to execute the Action, it sets a kind of try-catch mechanism with `On Error Resume Next`, as shown here:

```
' ----------------------------------
'--- Execute the Action
' ----------------------------------
On Error Resume Next
'--- Try
oAction.Run
' ----------------------------------
If Err.Number <> 0 Then 'Catch
  me.ErrorHandler.RunMappedProcedure(Err.Number)
End If
On Error Goto 0
```

So if an error occurs, it will be passed to `ErrorHandler` via the `RunMappedProcedure` method, and it will use either the specifically defined procedure for the error or the default procedure. This ensures that no exceptions will be left unhandled.

Building a test reporter

We have seen in the previous recipe that `Action` can accumulate data by adding information to its `Details` field. The `Status` field of `Action` is set from within the code, generally the `Run` method. Our reporting mechanism leverages the fact that the `Actions` are objects, and that they will use the native UFT reporter as their target output.

Getting ready

From the **File** menu, navigate to **New | Function Library**, or use the *Alt + Shift + N* shortcut. Save the file as `C:\Automation\Lib\lib.Reporter.vbs`.

How to do it...

Write the following code in the function library you created:

```
Function ReportActionStatus(ByRef p)
    ' -----------------------------------------------
    ' Function    :    ReportActionStatus
    ' Purpose     :    Reports an event to the UFT reporter with
    '   the data of the referenced Action
    ' Args        :    ByRef p
    ' Returns     :    N/A
```

```
    ' -------------------------------------------------
    Reporter.ReportEvent GetNormalizedStatus(p.Status.Value), _
        TypeName(p), p.Details & GetStatusText(p.Status.Value)
End Function


Function GetStatusText(ByVal iStatus)
    ' -------------------------------------------------
    ' Function    :    GetStatusText
    ' Purpose     :    Returns the text associated with a status
    ' Args        :    ByVal iStatus
    ' Returns     :    "success", "failure"
    ' -------------------------------------------------
    Dim sStatus

    Select Case CInt(iStatus)
        Case 0, 2, 4 'micPass, micDone, micInfo
            sStatus = "success"
        Case Else 'micFail, micWarning
            sStatus = "failure"
    End Select

    GetStatusText = sStatus
End Function


Function GetNormalizedStatus(ByVal iStatus)
    ' -------------------------------------------------
    ' Function    :    GetNormalizedStatus
    ' Purpose     :    Returns the status as 0 or 1
    ' Args        :    ByVal iStatus
    ' Returns     :    0 or 1
    ' -------------------------------------------------
    GetNormalizedStatus = micPass
    If CLng(iStatus) <> CLng(micPass) Then
        GetNormalizedStatus = micFail
    End If
End Function
```

The main function here is `ReportActionStatus`, which accepts the reference to an object that is built with the action design pattern and has both `Status` and `Details` as public fields.

The `GetStatusText` function is used to standardize the report message according to the status. The `GetNormalizedStatus` function limits the status to `0` (success) and `1` (failure), and it is used to standardize the accumulated statuses that can be sent from an Action or other function.

Finally, the `PrintReportInfo` function is just used to log messages to the UFT Reporter without affecting the results, as shown:

```
Function PrintReportInfo(ByVal sSender, ByVal sMessage)
    ' --------------------------------------------------
    ' Function    :     PrintReportInfo
    ' Purpose     :     Reports an info event to the UFT reporter
      and log
    ' Args        :     ByVal sSender
    '                   ByVal sMessage
    ' Returns     :     N/A
    ' --------------------------------------------------
    Print sSender & ": " & sMessage
    Reporter.ReportEvent micInfo, sSender, sMessage
End Function
```

How it works...

The `ReportActionStatus` function accepts the reference to an `Action` type object, which implements the design pattern as defined. With this reference, it has access to the public fields of `Action`, and so it retrieves and formats the data before sending it to the UFT reporter. This way, we make the reporting easier, as `Action` can just accumulate what it finds and the actual reporting in a single step.

Design Patterns

In this appendix, we will cover additional design patterns:

- ▶ Auxiliary classes and functions
- ▶ Action patterns
- ▶ Runtime data patterns

Auxiliary classes and functions

The following are auxiliary classes and functions' design patterns that provide additional functionality (not included within the main chapters):

- ▶ `AssertResult`: This design pattern checks whether the result triggers a predefined action:

```
Function ASSERT_RESULT(ByVal iResult)
    ' -----------------------------------------------------
    ---
    ' Function    :    ASSERT_RESULT
    ' Purpose     :    Checks if the result triggers a
    predefined action
    ' Args        :    ByVal iResult
    ' Returns     :    The value of iResult (unless the run
    session is
    '                     terminated)
    ' -----------------------------------------------------
    ---
    ASSERT_RESULT = CLng(iResult)
```

```
            If CLng(iResult) <> CLng(micPass) Then
                Reporter.ReportEvent micWarning, "ASSERT_RESULT",
                    "The action stopped by ASSERT_RESULT"
                Execute(Environment("ON_FAILURE") & "(" &
                    CStr(CLng(iResult)) & ")")
            End If
        End Function
```

▶ `InfoClassInstance`: This design pattern prints a log message relating to the instance of an object:

```
    Function InfoClassInstance(ByVal p, ByVal msg)
        '-----------------------------------------------------
         ---
        'Description:    Prints a log message relating to an
          object
        'Arguments    :
        '                  p - a reference to the instance
        '                  msg - a string
        'Usage        :    For example, in a Sub
          Class_Initialize within a Class
        '                  InfoClassInstance(me, "Loaded
          successfully")
        'Changes Log:
        '-----------------------------------------------------
         ---
        Print C_OBJ_OF_CLASS_MSG & typename(p) & msg & " at " &
          Timestamp()
    End Function
```

▶ `GetClassInstance`: The following design pattern returns an instance of a specific class:

```
    Function GetClassInstance(oInst, ByVal sClass)
        ' -----------------------------------------------------
         ---
        ' Function    :    GetClassInstance
        ' Purpose     :    Returns an instance of the specified
          Class
        ' Args        :    byRef oInst (output variable to
          return the instance)
        '                  ByVal sClass (name of requested Class)
        ' Returns     :    0 (success), 1 (failure)
        ' -----------------------------------------------------
         ---
        GetClassInstance = 0
        On Error Resume Next
        Execute "Set oInst = new " & sClass
```

```
          If Err.Number <> 0 Then
              Set oInst = Nothing
              GetClassInstance = 1
              reporter.ReportEvent micFail, "GetClassInstance",
                "Failed to create an instance of '" & sClass &
                "'"
          End If
      End Function
```

▶ GetIterations: This design pattern returns with a list of iterations for an array:

```
Function GetIterations(ByVal sIterations)
    ' -----------------------------------------------------
    ' -------------
    ' Function   :    GetIterations
    ' Purpose    :    Get array with list of iterations
    ' Args       :       ByVal sIterations - A comma and
      hyphen separated
    '                    string list with numbers of
      iterations to be run
    ' Returns    :     A System.Collections.ArrayList
    ' -----------------------------------------------------
    ' -------------
    ' Usage      :     Set DotNetArray =
      GetIterations("1,3,7-9,15-22")
    '                    Print DotNetArray.Count
    '                    For each item in DotNetArray
    '                        Print item
    '                    Next
    ' -----------------------------------------------------
    ' -------------
    Dim arrRange, min, max, i, j
    Dim arrIterations   : Set arrIterations =
      CreateObject("System.Collections.ArrayList")
    Dim arrTmp          : arrTmp = Split(sIterations,
      ",")

    'Parse array with iterations
    For i = 0 To Ubound(arrTmp)
        arrRange = Split(arrTmp(i), "-")

        If UBound(arrRange) = 1 Then '--- If is a Range
            min = arrRange(0)
            max = arrRange(1)
            If min > max Then
                Call SwapArgs(min, max)
```

```
                    End If

                    For j = min To max
                        arrIterations.Add j
                    Next
                Else '--- A single numeric value
                    arrIterations.Add arrTmp(i)
                End If
                '--- Dispose of temporary range array
                Erase arrRange
            Next
            '--- Dispose of temporary array
            Erase arrTmp
            '--- Return DotNet array
            Set GetIterations = arrIterations
        End Function
        ' -------------------------------------------------
```

▶ PadNumber: This design pattern pads a number string with zeros:

```
Function PadNumber(iNum, ByVal iMax)
        ' -----------------------------------------------------
        ---
        ' Function   :      PadNumber
        ' Purpose    :      Pad a number with zeroes
        ' Args       :       ByRef iNum (the number to be padded)
        '                    ByVal iMax (the max value of the
          range)
        ' Usage      :       PadNumber(3, 100) will return the
          string "003"
        ' Returns    :      String
        ' -----------------------------------------------------
        ---
        'Validates the arguments - If invalid Then it returns
          the value as is
        If (Not IsNumeric(iNum) or Not IsNumeric(iMax)) Then
            PadNumber = iNum
            Exit Function
        End If
        If (Abs(iNum) >= Abs(iMax)) Then
            PadNumber = iNum
            Exit Function
        End If

        PadNumber = String(Len(CStr(Abs(iMax)))-
          Len(CStr(Abs(iNum))), "0") & CStr(Abs(iNum))
End Function
```

▶ `Timestamp`: This design pattern returns a time stamped string:

```
Function Timestamp()
    ' ------------------------------------------------------
      ---
    ' Function   :    Timestamp
    ' Purpose    :    Build a timestamp string
    ' Args       :    N/A
    ' Returns    :    String
    ' ------------------------------------------------------
      ---
    dim sDate, sTime
    sDate=Date()
    sTime=Time()
    Timestamp = Year(sDate) & _
                PadNumber(Month(sDate), 12) & _
                PadNumber(Day(sDate), 31) & "_" & _
                PadNumber(Hour(sTime),24) & _
                PadNumber(Minute(sTime), 60) & _
                PadNumber(Second(sTime), 60)
End Function
```

▶ `CNum`: This design pattern returns values based on coalescing operators:

```
Class CNum
    Private m_value

    Public Function [=](n)
        value = n
    End Function
    Public Function [++]()
        value = value+1
        [++] = value
    End Function

    Public Function [--]()
        value = value-1
        [--] = value
    End Function
    Public Function [+=](n)
        value = value+n
        [+=] = value
    End Function
    Public Function [-=](n)
        value = value-n
        [-=] = value
```

```
            End Function
            Public Function [*=](n)
                value = value*n
                [*=] = value
            End Function
            Public Function [/=](n)
                value = value/n
                [/=] = value
            End Function
            Public Function [\=](n)
                value = value\n
                [\=] = value
            End Function
            public default Property Get Value()
                Value = m_value
            End Property
            public Property Let Value(n)
                m_value = n
            End Property
            sub class_initialize()
                value = 0
            End sub
        End Class
```

▶ [As Num]: This design pattern returns a string as a number:

```
Function [As Num](n)
    Set [As Num] = new CNum
    If isnumeric(n) Then [As Num].Value = n
End Function
```

▶ [++]: This design pattern returns an incremented string number value:

```
Function [++](n)
    Dim i
    Set i = [As Num](n)
    i.value = n
    i.[++]
    [++] = i
End Function
```

▶ [--]: This design pattern returns a decremented string number value:

```
Function[--](n)
    Dim i
    Set i = [As Num](n)
    i.value = n
    i.[--]
    [--] = i
End Function
```

Action patterns

The following action patterns provide sample Actions that can be executed within UFT:

▶ DoSomething: This design pattern calls the TimeStamp() function and prints the returned value:

```
Function DoSomething()
    Print "Doing something at " & Timestamp()
    DoSomething = 0
End Function
```

▶ [OpenApp]: This design pattern calls the preceding DoSomething() function combined with auxiliary classes and functions taken from the previous section to provide a reusable Action to provide a basic open AUT functionality:

```
Class [OpenApp]
    ' -------------------------------------------------
    ' Reusable Action: OpenApp
    ' Description:
    ' -------------------------------------------------
    Public Status
    Public Iteration
    Public StepNum
    Public dt
    Public Details

    Public Function Run()
        me.Details = "Ended with "
        me.Status.[=]0
        '--- TODO: The code
        me.Status.[+=]DoSomething()
```

```
                    '--- Report
                    Call ReportActionStatus(me)
            End Function


            Private Sub Class_Initialize
                    Call InfoClassInstance(me, C_OBJ_LOADED_MSG)
                    Set me.Status = [As Num](0)
            End Sub
            Private Sub Class_Terminate
                    Call InfoClassInstance(me, C_OBJ_UNLOADED_MSG)
                    Set me.Status = Nothing
            End Sub
    End Class
```

▶ [Login]: This design pattern provides a reusable Action for the target AUT in order
to provide a basic login/logon functionality:

```
Class [Login]
    ' ------------------------------------------------
    ' Reusable Action: Login
    ' Description: Login to the application
    ' ------------------------------------------------
    Public Status
    Public Iteration
    Public StepNum
    Public dt
    Public Details

    Public Function Run()
            me.Details = "Ended with "
            me.Status.[=]0
            '---
            me.Status.[+=]EnterUsername()
            me.Status.[+=]EnterPassword()
            me.Status.[+=]ClickOnLoginButton()

            '--- Report
            Call ReportActionStatus(me)
    End Function

    Function EnterUsername()
'           EnterUsername = me.Parent.WebEdit("txtUsername").
                Set(dt.GetParameter("USERNAME"))
    End Function
```

```
        Function EnterPassword()
'           EnterPassword = me.Parent.WebEdit("txtPassword")
                .Set(dt.GetParameter("PASSWORD"))
        End Function

        Function ClickOnLoginButton()
'           ClickOnLoginButton =
                me.Parent.WebButton("btnLogin").Click
        End Function

        Property Get Parent()
            Set Parent = Browser("MyStore").Page("Main")
        End Property

        Private Sub Class_Initialize
            Call InfoClassInstance(me, C_OBJ_LOADED_MSG)
            Set me.Status = [As Num](0)
        End Sub
        Private Sub Class_Terminate
            Call InfoClassInstance(me, C_OBJ_UNLOADED_MSG)
            Set me.Status = Nothing
        End Sub
    End Class
```

▶ [Search]: This design pattern provides a reusable Action for the target AUT in order to provide a basic search functionality:

```
Class [Search]
    ' -------------------------------------------------
    ' Reusable Action: Search
    ' Description:
    ' -------------------------------------------------
    Public Status
    Public Iteration
    Public StepNum
    Public dt
    Public Details

    Public Function Run()
        me.Details = "Ended with "
        me.Status.[=]0
        '--- TODO: The code
        me.Status.[+=]DoSomething()

        '--- Report
```

```
            Call ReportActionStatus(me)
        End Function

    Private Sub Class_Initialize
        Call InfoClassInstance(me, C_OBJ_LOADED_MSG)
        Set me.Status = [As Num](0)
    End Sub
    Private Sub Class_Terminate
        Call InfoClassInstance(me, C_OBJ_UNLOADED_MSG)
        Set me.Status = Nothing
    End Sub
End Class
```

▶ [AddToCart]: This design pattern provides a reusable Action in order to provide a
basic add to cart functionality for the target AUT:

```
Class [AddToCart]
    ' -----------------------------------------------
    ' Reusable Action: AddToCart
    ' Description:
    ' -----------------------------------------------
    Public Status
    Public Iteration
    Public StepNum
    Public dt
    Public Details

    Public Function Run()
        me.Details = "Ended with "
        me.Status.[=]0
        '--- TODO: The code
        me.Status.[+=]DoSomething()

        PrintReportInfo TypeName(me), "Added to cart: '" &
          dt.GetParameter("PRODUCT_NAME") & "'"

        '--- Report
        Call ReportActionStatus(me)
    End Function

    Private Sub Class_Initialize
        Call InfoClassInstance(me, C_OBJ_LOADED_MSG)
        Set me.Status = [As Num](0)
    End Sub
    Private Sub Class_Terminate
```

```
            Call InfoClassInstance(me, C_OBJ_UNLOADED_MSG)
            Set me.Status = Nothing
        End Sub
    End Class
```

▶ [Checkout]: This design pattern provides a reusable Action in order to provide a basic checkout functionality for the target AUT:

```
Class [Checkout]
    ' -------------------------------------------------
    ' Reusable Action: Checkout
    ' Description:
    ' -------------------------------------------------
    Public Status
    Public Iteration
    Public StepNum
    Public dt
    Public Details

    Public Function Run()
        me.Details = "Ended with "
        me.Status.[=]0
        '--- TODO: The code
        me.Status.[+=]DoSomething()

        '--- Report
        Call ReportActionStatus(me)
    End Function

    Private Sub Class_Initialize
        Call InfoClassInstance(me, C_OBJ_LOADED_MSG)
        Set me.Status = [As Num](0)
    End Sub
    Private Sub Class_Terminate
        Call InfoClassInstance(me, C_OBJ_UNLOADED_MSG)
        Set me.Status = Nothing
    End Sub
End Class
```

▶ [Logout]: This design pattern provides a reusable Action in order to provide a basic logout functionality for the target AUT:

```
Class [Logout]
    ' -------------------------------------------------
    ' Reusable Action: Logout
    ' Description:
```

```
' -----------------------------------------------
Public Status
Public Iteration
Public StepNum
Public dt
Public Details

Public Function Run()
    me.Details = "Ended with "
    me.Status.[=]0
    '--- TODO: The code
    me.Status.[+=]DoSomething()

  '--- Raise an error on purpose to show the Error
    Handler in action
    On Error Resume Next
    Err.Raise 9

    '--- Report
    Call ReportActionStatus(me)
End Function

Private Sub Class_Initialize
    Call InfoClassInstance(me, C_OBJ_LOADED_MSG)
    Set me.Status = [As Num](0)
End Sub
Private Sub Class_Terminate
    Call InfoClassInstance(me, C_OBJ_UNLOADED_MSG)
    Set me.Status = Nothing
End Sub
End Class
```

▶ [CloseApp]: This design pattern provides a reusable Action in order to provide a basic close functionality to the target AUT:

```
Class CloseApp
    ' -----------------------------------------------
    ' Reusable Action: CloseApp
    ' Description:
    ' -----------------------------------------------
    Public Status
    Public Iteration
    Public StepNum
    Public dt
    Public Details
```

```
Public Function Run()
    me.Details = "Ended with "
    me.Status.[=]0
    '--- TODO: The code
    me.Status.[+=]DoSomething()

    '--- Report
    Call ReportActionStatus(me)
End Function

Private Sub Class_Initialize
    Call InfoClassInstance(me, C_OBJ_LOADED_MSG)
    Set me.Status = [As Num](0)
End Sub
Private Sub Class_Terminate
    Call InfoClassInstance(me, C_OBJ_UNLOADED_MSG)
    Set me.Status = Nothing
End Sub
End Class
```

Runtime data patterns

The following runtime data patterns provide sample datasheets to be consumed within UFT:

▶ Steps: This runtime data pattern provides the sample datasheet required for execution of the Action patterns, described in the previous section as the master driver file:

STEP_ID	ACTION_NAME	RUN	DATASHEET	ITERATIONS	ON_FAILURE
10	OpenApp	TRUE	N/A		ExitTest
20	Login	TRUE			ExitTest
30	Search	TRUE			ExitAction
40	AddToCart	TRUE		1 to 3	ExitAction
50	Checkout	TRUE			ExitAction
60	Logout	TRUE	N/A		ExitAction
70	CloseApp	TRUE	N/A		ExitTest

▶ `Login`: This runtime data pattern provides the sample datasheet required for the execution of Action `[Login]`, described in the previous section as the master data file:

USERNAME	PASSWORD
User1	53d3905671ff1996dc6d1b4399eb

▶ `Search`: This runtime data pattern provides the sample datasheet required for execution of Action `[Search]`, described in the previous section as the master data file:

SEARCH_TERM
Book

▶ `AddToCart`: This runtime data pattern provides the sample datasheet required for execution of Action `[AddToCart]`, described in the previous section as the master data file:

PRODUCT_NAME
My Book 1
My Book 2
My Book 3

▶ `Checkout`: This runtime data pattern provides the sample datasheet required for execution of Action `[Checkout]`, described in the previous section as the master data file:

CREDIT_CARD	CCV	EXPIRATION_DATE	CUSTOMER_ID
999999999999	999	31/12/2017	999999999

Index

Thank you for buying
Advanced UFT 12 for Test Engineers Cookbook

About Packt Publishing

Packt, pronounced 'packed', published its first book "*Mastering phpMyAdmin for Effective MySQL Management*" in April 2004 and subsequently continued to specialize in publishing highly focused books on specific technologies and solutions.

Our books and publications share the experiences of your fellow IT professionals in adapting and customizing today's systems, applications, and frameworks. Our solution-based books give you the knowledge and power to customize the software and technologies you're using to get the job done. Packt books are more specific and less general than the IT books you have seen in the past. Our unique business model allows us to bring you more focused information, giving you more of what you need to know, and less of what you don't.

Packt is a modern, yet unique publishing company, which focuses on producing quality, cutting-edge books for communities of developers, administrators, and newbies alike. For more information, please visit our website: www.PacktPub.com.

About Packt Enterprise

In 2010, Packt launched two new brands, Packt Enterprise and Packt Open Source, in order to continue its focus on specialization. This book is part of the Packt Enterprise brand, home to books published on enterprise software – software created by major vendors, including (but not limited to) IBM, Microsoft and Oracle, often for use in other corporations. Its titles will offer information relevant to a range of users of this software, including administrators, developers, architects, and end users.

Writing for Packt

We welcome all inquiries from people who are interested in authoring. Book proposals should be sent to author@packtpub.com. If your book idea is still at an early stage and you would like to discuss it first before writing a formal book proposal, contact us; one of our commissioning editors will get in touch with you.

We're not just looking for published authors; if you have strong technical skills but no writing experience, our experienced editors can help you develop a writing career, or simply get some additional reward for your expertise.

Designing and Implementing Test Automation Frameworks with QTP

ISBN: 978-1-78217-102-7   Paperback: 160 pages

Learn how to design and implement a test automation framework block by block

1. A simple and easy demonstration of the important concepts will enable you to translate abstract ideas into practice.

2. Each chapter begins with an outline and a brief statement of content to help the reader establish perspective.

3. An alternative approach to developing generic components for test automation.

Designing and Implementing Test Automation Frameworks with QTP

Ashish Bhargava

Instant Selenium Testing Tools Starter

ISBN: 978-1-78216-514-9   Paperback: 52 pages

A short, fast, and focused guide to Selenium Testing tools that delivers immediate results

1. Learn something new in an Instant! A short, fast, focused guide delivering immediate results.

2. Learn to create web tests using Selenium Tools.

3. Learn to use Page Object Pattern.

4. Run and analyze test results on an easy-to-use platform.

Selenium Testing Tools Starter

A short, fast, and focused guide to Selenium Testing tools that delivers immediate results

Unmesh Gundecha

Please check **www.PacktPub.com** for information on our titles

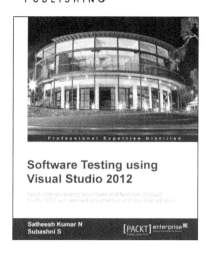

Software Testing using Visual Studio 2012

ISBN: 978-1-84968-954-0   Paperback: 444 pages

Learn different testing techniques and features of Visual Studio 2012 with detailed explanations and real-time samples

1. Using Test Manager and managing test cases and test scenarios.

2. Exploratory testing using Visual Studio 2012.

3. Learn unit testing features and coded user interface testing.

Selenium Testing Tools Cookbook

ISBN: 978-1-84951-574-0   Paperback: 326 pages

Over 90 recipes to build, maintain, and improve test automation with Selenium WebDriver

1. Learn to leverage the power of Selenium WebDriver with simple examples that illustrate real-world problems and their workarounds.

2. Each sample demonstrates key concepts allowing you to advance your knowledge of Selenium WebDriver in a practical and incremental way.

3. Explains testing of mobile web applications with Selenium drivers for platforms such as iOS and Android.

Please check **www.PacktPub.com** for information on our titles

www.ingramcontent.com/pod-product-compliance
Lightning Source LLC
LaVergne TN
LVHW062310060326
832902LV00013B/2140

9 781849 688406